P_i

BEHAVIOUR BUSINESS

"A breath of fresh air – a brilliant behavioural science book that focuses on the practical application of the topic rather than the abstract theories."

RICHARD SHOTTON
Author of *The Choice Factory*

"The better you are at understanding and influencing behaviour, the better you'll be at business. This book is a must read for anyone who has a business/cause/brand to grow … It's engaging, easy to read, has many applied examples and strong theoretical underpinnings. Read it now before you miss out."

ADAM FERRIER
Founder Thinkerbell, author of *The Advertising Effect: How to change behaviour*,
Australian media commentator and writer (*Gruen*, *TIME*, *The Guardian*)

"Richard Chataway's fine book attests to the power and profit of behavioural science in business … on offer are effective behavioural solutions for all business types and sizes – practical and low-cost applications, honed over many years by a foremost practitioner of behavioural science."

PHILIP CORR
Professor of Psychology and Behavioural Economics/Science at City, University of London, co-author *Behavioral Economics: The Basics*

"If you buy one business book this year, make this the one. A handbook on how to apply behavioural science the right way for your business … the perfect guide for anyone who is looking to up their game in 2020 and beyond."

PAUL ARMSTRONG
Founder of emerging technology consultancy Here/Forth, journalist for *Forbes*,
Reuters, and *Evening Standard*, and author of *Disruptive Technologies*

Every owner of a physical copy of this edition of

The
BEHAVIOUR
BUSINESS

can download the eBook for free direct from us at
Harriman House, in a DRM-free format that can be read on
any eReader, tablet or smartphone.

Simply head to:

ebooks.harriman-house.com/
behaviourbusiness

to get your copy now.

The
BEHAVIOUR
BUSINESS

How to apply behavioural science for business success

RICHARD CHATAWAY

Foreword by **RORY SUTHERLAND**,
*TED talk superstar and vice-chairman of
Ogilvy Group UK*

HARRIMAN HOUSE LTD
3 Viceroy Court
Petersfield
Hampshire
GU32 3LJ
GREAT BRITAIN
Tel: +44 (0)1730 233870

Email: enquiries@harriman-house.com
Website: harriman.house

First published in Great Britain in 2020.
Copyright © Richard Chataway 2020.

The right of Richard Chataway to be identified as the Author has been asserted in accordance with the Copyright, Design and Patents Act 1988.

Paperback ISBN: 978-0-85719-734-4
eBook ISBN: 978-0-85719-735-1

British Library Cataloguing in Publication Data
A CIP catalogue record for this book can be obtained from the British Library.

Contents

About the Author

RICHARD CHATAWAY is vice president of BVA Nudge Unit UK and founder of Communication Science Group (CSG), and one of the most experienced behavioural science practitioners in the UK. He has worked in senior strategic roles for government in Australia and the UK, and for the four largest advertising agency groups, addressing behavioural challenges as varied as getting people to stop smoking, join the armed forces, drink spirits rather than wine, prevent domestic violence, pay for university tuition, submit their taxes, buy flatpack furniture, and take public transport – to name a few.

He has advised clients including Lloyds Banking Group, Google, Atos, IKEA and ITV, and conducted training for call-centre personnel, marketing directors, sales teams, creatives, and everything in between.

Richard is a frequent conference speaker and board member of the Association for Business Psychology, the industry body that is the home and voice of business psychology in the UK.

Preface

What this book is about

The Behaviour Business is about practically applying behavioural science in business.

It is intended to be an illuminating guide to how behavioural science can help us answer the key challenges facing business today – and why every business, big or small, needs to truly understand behaviour to succeed.

If you are looking for a comprehensive academic guide to behavioural science theory, this book is not it.

Aside from a brief part of chapter 1, this book will not explain in detail concepts and theories from behavioural science, nor will it give a list of the different heuristics, biases and fallacies that seek to explain the curiosities of human behaviour. Fascinating though these are, you do not need a MSc in psychology to read this book.

Who this book is for

My intention is that this book can be used by *anyone* who wants to understand how to apply the powerful insights of behavioural science to help them in business. It's an exciting new discipline which can help you overcome challenges in a huge number of areas: customer experience, marketing, consumer research, retention, recruitment, performance, artificial intelligence or automation, and more.

I have learnt a lot from a wide range of experts – through interview, working with them directly, and exploring their key works – to bring you the latest and best insights.

Whether you are a manager, marketer, consultant, entrepreneur, student or salesperson, if you are in business (or have ambitions to be) and are curious about being more successful at influencing the behaviour of yourself and others for business success, then this book is for you.

How this book is structured

Each part of the book seeks to address a different challenge facing modern businesses. These parts are broken down into four chapters, three that explore a different aspect of the challenge, before a conclusion with key recommendations on what to do now to benefit from these insights. Fascinating theories, experiments and concepts from behavioural science are used throughout – these are taken both from my own work and leading academics and practitioners.

Where these concepts are particularly important, they are explained in separate sections with examples. If you want to learn more about the science, references and suggestions for further reading are included throughout the book.

Part one introduces the key concepts of behavioural science, how they have been used to change the behaviour of citizens and how they can (and should) be applied in business. Part two examines how the most successful businesses of the 21st century have used behavioural science to deliver digital products and services. Next, part three looks at how behavioural science can help businesses successfully use the concomitant advances in technology to make business work for humans, as well as robots. Part four looks at how to use behavioural science to recruit, retain and motivate the humans that work in your business. Part five shows how a deeper understanding of human behaviour helps you know what your customers want – and don't want. And finally, part six explores how to successfully influence the behaviour of those customers – the goal of marketing – before a brief conclusion to reflect on the key themes, and the future.

A final note: I have made extensive use of footnotes. These are intended as asides, additional explanations, trivia and references for those who wish to read more.[1] Should you wish, you can happily ignore them.

---

1 They also stop me from rambling or going off on unnecessary tangents. Like this one.

Foreword
by Rory Sutherland

W E SHAPE OUR tools and then our tools shape us.

For the last few decades, aided and accelerated by the invention of the spreadsheet, businesses and public sector organisations have become disproportionately obsessed with measurement and quantification. There is no activity which is not judged on 'key metrics' or which is not subject to regular measurement and comparison.

'What gets measured gets managed', as the phrase goes.

Hours are duly spent in defining these measures and in devising ways to 'improve' them. In time, this results in more and more perverse behaviour, as people run out of good ideas and learn to game the system instead – since anything that improves a metric is rewarded. Highly intelligent people are strangely susceptible to this failing. Recently it was revealed that Ivy League universities were in the habit of encouraging applications from potential candidates who had no hope of being accepted. The reason? By rejecting these candidates' applications, the university could improve its 'selectivity stats' by allowing it to claim that it accepted a smaller percentage of applicants than its competitors, hence burnishing its elite credentials. It seems almost unbelievable that, in the pursuit of improving a measure, leading universities could engage in the hideous practice of falsely raising the hopes of thousands of young people before dashing them. Tragically this is exactly what they did.

The practitioners of this kind of 'McKinsey Capitalism' usually think themselves great believers in free markets. And it never occurs to them that there is a whiff of Stalinism about this obsession with statistics, and with the pursuit of false proxy targets at any cost. (At one point, chandeliers in the Soviet Union posed a significant health hazard, since the factory was rewarded on the weight of its output – and had responded by producing light-fittings of such extraordinary heft that ceilings were often at risk of collapse.)

❝ the pursuit of rational, objective and quantifiable metrics only makes sense if these are closely aligned with the things that your customers care about ❞

But this is not confined to communism. In fact, any managerial or bureaucratic culture has an incentive to engage in over-measurement, since the act of quantification allows the manager or bureaucrat to present their decision-making as being rational and objective, and thereby sidestep the risk of blame. The reason this causes problems is that the pursuit of rational, objective and quantifiable metrics only makes sense if these are closely aligned with the things that your customers care about. More and more evidence from behavioural science and behavioural economics suggests that this is a very unsafe assumption. In fact, what consumers care about may have very little to do with the objective qualities of a product or service, and their preferences may differ markedly from those of the representative, single, utility-maximising rational agent who populates all economic models.

Making decisions on this basis alone may be good for the manager's career prospects – but commercially disastrous. Not only does it fail to deliver what consumers really value, but it makes you more and more similar in your decision-making to your think-alike rational competitors.

What gets mismeasured gets mismanaged.

The licence given to businesses by mainstream economics to make decisions while effectively ignoring psychological or perceptual factors is doubly disastrous for business decision-making: it focuses companies on improving the wrong things, and, by assuming consumers to be rational maximisers, it limits the notion of what improvements and innovations might most motivate different customers, who may be highly different in their preferences. It is hence creatively limiting.

To redress this imbalance, marketers and other imaginative business innovators need to use the methodology and vocabulary of behavioural economics to start to win arguments in the boardroom. They need to develop proper new metrics to complement the objective metrics which have become overused. Instead of measuring the length of queues or the overcrowding on trains, they need to measure the irritation of waiting or the level of inconvenience endured. It will take time to redress the balance – but thanks to books like this it is starting to happen.

RORY SUTHERLAND
London, 2020

Introduction

If you are in business, you are in the business of behaviour.

Unless a business influences behaviour, it will not succeed. A business needs people to buy and use its products and services to generate revenue. It needs people to make and deliver those products and services.

Or at the very least it needs people to create those products and services, or to build and program the machines that create them. And it needs to do those things better than its competitors to survive and grow.

This much should be self-evident. But there are lots of things businesses do that fly in the face of the latest evidence on how, and why, people behave as they do. Or worse, businesses frequently don't even try to change behaviour, but merely perceptions or attitudes, and wrongly assume behaviour will follow.

If there is one thing to learn from behavioural science, it is this: what people do is *often not the same as what they say they do, or intend to.* If a business does not employ this understanding of how people make decisions – that they are frequently driven by subconscious or external factors they are not aware of – they are wasting the business's money (and that of any shareholders).

The good news is that in the last 50 years we have learnt more about how, and why, people behave as they do than we learnt in the previous 5,000. Like advances in medicine, technology, and computing, the growth of knowledge in behavioural science has been extraordinary. It has been driven by academic disciplines like behavioural economics, social/evolutionary psychology and neuroscience, and the work of a number of dedicated practitioners.[2]

---

2   An important note on terminology. I use the term behavioural science in this book, rather than behavioural economics or social psychology (for example), because the insights used in this book come from a variety of disciplines such as those mentioned, and I find it is the best term to encapsulate a holistic study of human decision-making. Also, as we will see, a scientific approach is critical to effectively applying these insights.

A number of leading thinkers referenced in this book are now key advisors to governments and businesses around the world. Similarly, two key luminaries – Professors Daniel Kahneman and Richard Thaler – have been awarded Nobel Prizes this century.

There is much for businesses to learn.

But this is not a guide to the science, nor a list of biases or irrationalities in human behaviour, because (*whisper*), confession time: I am not a behavioural scientist – despite often being introduced as such (or a behavioural economist or psychologist) when I am speaking at conferences.

I am a practitioner.

My career has been based on *applying* the insights from behavioural science to influence behaviour. My knowledge and passion for the subject is entirely derived from a career which has focused on harnessing insights from this discipline in the private and public sectors.

A deeper understanding of behaviour can help you achieve a far greater impact. When I was working at the UK Department of Health, our head of anti-smoking policy once told the team we could potentially save more lives in a year than many surgeons do in their entire careers. It was then I realised the potential to change behaviour at scale by better understanding the real drivers of behaviour.

It also became clear to me that the ways in which the public sector used behavioural insights to help people lead longer, happier lives could equally be applied to other challenges.

Some of the behavioural challenges I have addressed include getting people to: stop smoking; join the armed forces; drink spirits rather than wine; pay for university tuition; submit their taxes; work more collaboratively; build flatpack furniture; complete their timesheets; and take public transport – as well as buy numerous products and services.

Developing a behaviourally informed strategy enabled my colleagues and I to win a global campaign of the year award in 2014 for a social media campaign addressing domestic violence. It also led to the development of the world's most successful stop-smoking mobile app: My QuitBuddy. I have conducted training for call centre personnel, CEOs, marketing directors, creatives, TV continuity announcers, customer experience directors, university administrators and pretty much everything in between. I have briefed ministers of state, advised financial technology start-ups, and spoken at conferences of health workers, business psychologists and nutritionists.

The only way I have been able to have such a varied career is because I have been fortunate enough to study, read and collaborate with many more qualified people. You will see many of them listed in the acknowledgements – this book represents their thoughts as much as mine. In compiling this book, I interviewed 25 of the most inspirational and thoughtful practitioners to benefit from their best practice.

In these conversations I found that there was something all the leading practitioners had in common. Despite disparate academic and career backgrounds, they all shared an innate curiosity to understand how the mind works. They are eager to know why people behave in ways that might not initially make sense, to challenge conventional wisdom, and build better businesses as a result – just as we make progress in science. As Einstein said: "The important thing is not to stop questioning. Curiosity has its own reason for existing."

Should you want to hear more from them, please listen to the podcast series that accompanies this book – and seek out as many books, blogs, tweets and utterings from these luminaries as you can.

One final thought before you dive into the wonderful world of behavioural science in business: these tools for influencing are more powerful than many realise. Recent global events are making this increasingly plain. The ethical risks raised by the application of behavioural science are important and will be addressed throughout the book.

My inspiration to pursue a career in applied behavioural science was derived from seeing its potential to help people make the decisions they want to make, and to help businesses fashion workplaces, products and services that improve our lives and contribute to the economy.

To make our lives better, not worse.

Now, let's get down to business.

PART
ONE

How to Create
a Behavioural Business

CHAPTER I
Undoing Economics –
A New Way of Thinking

Undoing economics

W HEN I WAS at university 20 years ago, behavioural science as a
field of study was virtually non-existent.

But now, things are very different. In addition to flourishing academic
courses on behavioural science, behavioural economics and experimental
psychology, there are over 200 behavioural insights teams operating with
local and national governments around the world. Leading companies are
installing chief behavioural officers, and working with businesses like my
own to embed this understanding into their work.

The history of behavioural science, and how it has led us to a richer,
more accurate understanding of what drives our behaviour, is really a classic
underdog story. It is the story of how the 300-year-old goliath of traditional
economic theory, which sees humans as rational operators, has been felled
by a group of determined academics – in particular the ground-breaking
work of Daniel Kahneman and Amos Tversky[3] – using the slingshot of
behavioural economics.

What is heartening is that this new way of thinking – that humans
are not purely rational, utility-maximising calculators, as neoclassical
economics often assumed – is fast becoming the norm. Forward-thinking

---

3   If you are interested in that story, and the people behind it, then I'd strongly recommend
reading Michael Lewis's account of the work and friendship of those two pioneers: *The
Undoing Project.*

governments around the world are embedding this approach into their policy. The world of business is actually lagging (badly) behind.

But times are changing. When running training courses in behavioural science, I like to gauge knowledge in the room by asking which of the leading popular science books on the topic (like *Thinking Fast and Slow* and *Nudge*) people have read. Ten years ago, between 10–20% of people in the room had one or more of those books. These days the ratio is usually over 50%, as the base level of knowledge has grown.

In addition to building that knowledge and understanding within a business, either by hiring those lucky enough to study it or buying it in from outside, what can a business do to ensure it is always focused on changing behaviour? And what, structurally and strategically, does focusing on behaviour mean in a business?

That is what we shall explore in this part of the book. But first, let's examine what is new about this way of thinking, and what it means for businesses in general.[4]

Why is behavioural science important for business?

After the 18th century,[5] academic theory about how people behaved was mostly based on a traditional economic theory of utility maximisation. That is, every human decision was based on a simple rational weighing up of the pros and cons of a particular action. Professors Richard Thaler and Cass Sunstein, the authors of *Nudge*, call this straw-man version of humans an 'econ', or *homo economicus* – because it is someone who only exists in the pages of an economics textbook. Like the character Spock from *Star Trek*, they are a totally rational operator, ungoverned by emotions.

And, like Spock, they are not human.

---

4   If you have read *Thinking Fast and Slow*, *Nudge* or other books, or have an academic background in behavioural science, then much of the following paragraphs will be familiar.
5   Largely based on the work of Swiss mathematician Daniel Bernouilli and expected utility theory. There is a lot of lively academic debate about how the seminal 18th-century economist, Adam Smith, was actually well aware of the irrationalities of human decision-making and incorporated it into his theories – what he called the 'passions' versus the 'impartial spectator' in *The Theory of Moral Sentiments*. But whether he was truly the first behavioural economist is outside the scope of this book.

Let's take an example – why people commit crime – to show the flaws of this approach. The University of Chicago economist and Nobel laureate Gary Becker devised what is known as the Simple Model of Rational Crime (SMORC) to explain why crime happens. This states that, in any given situation, a potential criminal weighs up the benefits of the crime (e.g. the financial gain) versus the potential costs (e.g. likelihood of being caught and going to jail).

According to this theory, the Enron fraudsters, for example, made this cost-benefit analysis and (wrongly with hindsight) decided the money they made was worth the risk of their actions. That risk being jail time and the future insolvency of the business.

The problem with SMORC, like most neoclassical economic theory (and financial models and management/marketing theory derived from it), is it assumes the Spock model of humans as totally rational beings who only act based on self-interest.

If this were true, all of us would be committing certain low-risk crimes on a daily basis. As Dan Ariely, James B. Duke Professor of Psychology and Behavioural Economics at Duke University writes:

"We wouldn't make decisions based on emotions or trust, so we would most likely lock our wallets in a drawer when we stepped out of our office for a minute … There would be no value in shaking hands as a form of agreement; legal contracts would be necessary for any transaction … We might decide not to have kids because when they grew up, they, too, would try to steal everything we have, and living in our homes gives them plenty of opportunities to do so."[6]

If you have ever tried to stop some form of dishonest behaviour in business – over-claiming on expenses, or stealing lunches from the communal fridge, for example – you will know this is not an accurate picture of how people behave. Increasing the chances of being caught (emailing the company saying you are checking expenses more thoroughly in future, for example)[7] will not solve the problem.

This is because emotions play a key part in decision-making: our behaviour is not just governed by financial benefit. Although it fell in 2018 to 72% from normal levels of 90%,[8] the murder detection rate in London

---

6   *The (Honest) Truth About Dishonesty*, Ariely D, Harper Collins (2012).

7   In this case, this possibly creates a negative social norm, explained on page 10.

8   www.theguardian.com/uk-news/2018/dec/12/london-homicides-now-highest-in-a-year-for-a-decade

is so high that no one would ever rationally consider it a wise course of action. Yet over 130 murders were committed in the capital that year, most of which had no obvious utility to the perpetrator. Clearly, there are other drivers of criminal behaviour.

Ariely's work has shown that emotions can be effectively used to combat dishonest and illegal behaviour. In one case, he reduced the proportion of over-claiming (cheating) made on a simple insurance form by 15%.

How? Simply by moving the standard 'I promise that the information I am providing is true' declaration from the end of the form, to the beginning. This made the honesty requirement more *salient*[9] – and made no difference to the costs or benefits of the crime.

This is one example of how social psychology, the discipline that looks at social interactions (i.e. how people behave in the real world as social beings) has given us insights into how external factors affect our behaviour. This gives us a better model of understanding how people make decisions – in particular that our behaviour is subject to many behavioural biases, and mental short-cuts, to help us navigate the world around us.

The genius of the work of Kahneman and Tversky (and others) was to start testing and codifying some of these biases – coining the term 'heuristics' to cover some of the most prevalent decision-making short-cuts – and then to devise a coherent model to explain why these heuristics lead us to often make non-rational, counter-intuitive or erroneous decisions.

In short, they told us how humans actually behave. And businesses are run for, by, and with humans – for the time being at least.

SOCIAL NORMS AND SOCIAL PROOF

Have you ever been in an unfamiliar place and been looking to find somewhere good to eat? Imagine you see two restaurants – both look reasonable, clean places, with good menus serving food you like.

One is busy, bustling and full of happy, laughing customers. The other has a sad-looking man in the window, eating alone. Which do you choose?

---

9 Explained on page 14.

Most of us would choose the former. This is an example of how social proof (our behavioural bias to look to others like us to validate our behaviour) and social norms (our perception of what most other people like us are doing) are powerful influences on our behaviour. If something is popular with our 'in-group', we desire it more. Even though, in this case, the second restaurant would serve us quicker and possibly give us better service, since they might be more grateful for the custom.

There is an evolutionary logic to this, as with most behavioural biases. Seeing others like us behaving in a certain way shows that it is a safe, validated and rewarding course of action. The restaurant must be good if all those other people are using it, right?

Most people are familiar with colloquial versions of this effect, like peer pressure and herd mentality, and the restaurant trade uses the effect better than most. A TripAdvisor certificate at the door showing a 5-star rating is leveraging social proof.[10]

Simply showing something is popular can influence behaviour. In 2010, Facebook deployed an 'I Voted' button (below) showing how many users had voted as part of a campaign to encourage turnout in the US Congressional election. Versions of the button, or no button at all, were shown to 61m people in a joint study by the University of California in San Diego and Facebook data scientists. They used voting records to determine the button's impact on real-world voting. It turns out the button's call to action increased the total vote count by 340,000 votes.

But more interestingly, the version of the button which showed whether the individual user's friends (i.e. people they actually knew)

---

10   Such is the influence of online review sites that restaurants, hotels etc. have become somewhat obsessed, and the system has been gamed by some unscrupulous practitioners. This was hilariously demonstrated in 2017 by *Vice* journalist Oobah Butler, who created a fake restaurant called The Shed at Dulwich, based at his garden shed in south-east London. Using his experiences writing fake reviews for £10 for real restaurants, he got his friends to write fake TripAdvisor reviews in sufficient volumes to become rated in the top 2,000 restaurants in London. As part of the hoax, he shot fake Instagram pictures of the food (including a ham hock that was actually a close up of his ankle) and created made-up dishes such as vegan clams. He leveraged scarcity bias (explained on page 29) by creating a phone number and website for appointment-only bookings (which was never answered). Despite not actually existing, it became the top-rated restaurant in London in 2017. Butler staged an opening night for the restaurant, serving thinly-disguised £1 ready meals to ten customers. Despite having been blindfolded and then led down the alley past his house to the end of the garden and the shed, some said they wanted to come back and would recommend it. (www.theshedatdulwich.com)

had voted was *four times* more effective than the version with just the 'I Voted' button and the total number. This demonstrates that to get the best out of social proof we need to consider who the most important influences are (in social psychology terms, defining the in-group).

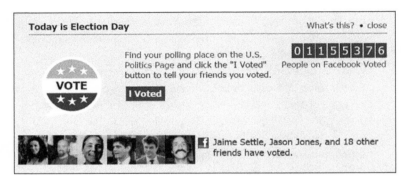

Source: Nature (www.nature.com/articles/489212a)

Care needs to be taken that highlighting bad behaviour doesn't have an unintended consequence of making it seem normal – known as negative social proof. For example, highlighting the amount of alcohol drunk by students on a university campus had the effect of increasing the perceived norm amongst students, leading to the average student drinking *more*.[11] It's not hard to see examples of this misapplication – a GP surgery putting up a sign saying that 200 people missed their appointments last month will likely increase the number of missed appointments next month, not decrease.

The solution is to use positive framing (e.g. 99% of our patients attend their appointments) or highlight the 'injunctive' norm (what people should do), rather than the 'descriptive' norm (what they actually do). Road signs say that the speed limit is 30mph – they don't tell you that most people actually drive at 35.

So next time you go to a quiet restaurant and are encouraged by a waiter to sit in the window (so others can see you) – you have experienced social proof in action.

---

11 citeseerx.ist.psu.edu/viewdoc/download?doi=10.1.1.470.522&rep=rep1&type=pdf

Two systems of thinking – designing for Homer

These heuristics and biases are important because we use them to help us make the thousands of decisions required every day.

"Many people are overconfident, prone to put too much faith in their intuitions," wrote Kahneman. "They apparently find cognitive effort at least mildly unpleasant and avoid it as much as possible."[12]

In short: we think less than we think we think. As Thaler and Sunstein put it, we are often less like Spock, and more like Homer Simpson.

Kahneman popularised the term 'system 1', or 'fast' thinking, to explain these instinctive, emotionally driven, less-conscious decision-making processes. Our more rational, 'slow' decision-making – which adheres more closely to the Spock view of behaviour – he called 'system 2'. Subsequently, behavioural scientists have identified the circumstances when we are in system-1 mode when making decisions, and (to date) over 200 different heuristics and biases that come into play.

The importance of this is twofold: one, we have chronically underestimated just how much of our decision-making is of this instinctive type, with some estimates indicating that it accounts for between 90–95% of our daily behaviour; two, that only by understanding these heuristics and biases can we effectively explain, influence and change behaviour.

We are more like Homer Simpson than we care to realise or admit. These behavioural biases are hugely important in determining how we behave, and perform an important function – not least because of our increasingly complicated lives, where we are often over-burdened with information and stimuli. Over the course of this book, we will see examples of how understanding biases can help us successfully address behavioural challenges.

This melding of psychological and economic thinking about behaviour, which became known as the discipline of behavioural economics, is the closest thing we have to a unifying theory of decision-making. In 2002, it earned Kahneman, a psychologist, the Nobel prize for economics.[13]

---

12   *Thinking Fast and Slow,* Kahneman D, Penguin (2011).
13   Undoubtedly his long-time friend and colleague Amos Tversky would have jointly been awarded this prize also, but he sadly died in 1996.

This work has shown that when considering influencing behaviour in business it is important to think about whether you are dealing with Homer or Spock. Because you will be dealing with Homer more often than you might realise.

AVAILABILITY BIAS AND SALIENCY

Availability bias is a phenomenon that explains a lot of human behaviour, particularly aspects that are obviously irrational. It reflects how our worldview is determined largely by the information available to us. As Daniel Kahneman puts it: in psychological terms, 'What You See Is All There Is' (WYSIATI). As a result we often overestimate the likelihood of events because they are more mentally available – that is, easier to bring to mind because they are easily remembered or particularly relevant to us.

The most obvious manifestation of this is phobias. What are you afraid of? Snakes or spiders perhaps? Arachnophobes like myself will explain our fear in all sorts of ways. Snakes are slimy (they're not), spiders are big and hairy and menacing (many are, but not the sort you meet in Uttoxeter).

The wealth of information now at our fingertips through the proliferation of news channels, the growth of the internet and so on has enhanced some of these biases. Unfortunately, humans tend to give more credence to information that confirms their existing views (as a result of confirmation bias, see page 143), and our demand for that information dictates the information available, in a vicious cycle of fear-mongering.

Have a look at the data overleaf. There is a huge difference between what actually is likely to kill us and what we think will kill us (and therefore worry about). The chart at the bottom shows what the media actually tells us to worry about. 'If it bleeds, it leads' as the old journalistic mantra has it – even in reputable news sources like the New York Times and Guardian. And so, our perceived risk of death by terrorism (for example) is unrealistically high as a result.

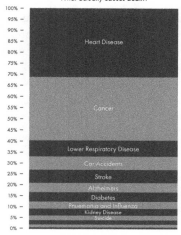

CDC Cause of Death in USA
"What actually causes death?"

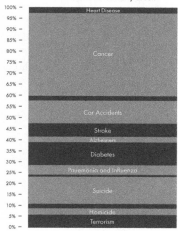

Google Search Trends
"Which causes do we worry about?"

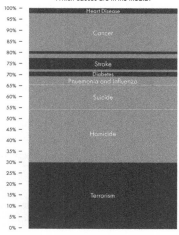

NYT & Guardian Headlines
"Which causes are in the media?"

Based on in-depth analysis by H. Al-Jamaly, M. Siemers,
O. Shen, and N. Stone at owenshen24.github.io/charting-death

Data: CDC, Google, New York Times, The Guardian
Code: www.github.com/aaronpenne
Twitter: @aaronpenne
Aaron Penne @2018

Source: Aaron Penne

Saliency is an important, related concept – things that are more relevant, noticeable and recent are more emotionally striking, and therefore more mentally available. "If you have personally experienced a serious earthquake, you're more likely to believe that an earthquake is likely than if you read about it in a weekly magazine," say Thaler and Sunstein in *Nudge*.

For businesses, mental availability is hugely important. If your products and services are easy to bring to mind, and you build the right associations with them, then you can more easily influence how people behave in relation to them. As we shall see in part six, this goes a long way to explaining how marketing and advertising actually works.

How behavioural science changes how we think about business decision-making

When Kahneman was in the Israeli Air Force during the turbulent 1960s (when Israel was in frequent, bloody armed conflict with its neighbours), he was working in a role commonly taken by psychologists in business today.[14] He was designing training and assessment to achieve the best possible performance from their staff – in this case, fighter pilots.

Instructors told him they believed criticism worked better than praise as a strategy to influence their students' behaviour. As Michael Lewis writes, "The pilot who was praised always performed worse the next time out, and the pilot who was criticised always performed better. Danny [Kahneman] watched for a bit and then explained to them what was actually going on: the pilot who was praised because he had flown exceptionally well, like the pilot who was chastised after he had flown exceptionally badly, simply were regressing to the mean. They'd have tended to perform better (or worse) even if the teacher had said nothing at all."[15]

That critical insight led Kahneman and Tversky to one of the key theories behind their model of how humans make decisions, specifically the representativeness heuristic.[16] Their psychologically informed way of

---

14   I am a board member for the Association for Business Psychology in the UK, and the majority of our members are business psychologists whose role at least partly involves assessing performance of people and teams in work.

15   *The Undoing Project*, Lewis, M, Penguin (2018).

16   This is where an event is assumed to be more likely because it shares characteristics of its category – even though this has no effect on likelihood. In this case, criticism led to a better performance, so the assumption was this was the cause and effect.

looking at behaviour shows us how behavioural science can change the way businesses approach problems, and the value of psychology in solving them.

Firstly, it tells us a lot about data. The data seemed to confirm that the actions of the teacher were working. They criticise, then the student performs better. But, as any statistician can tell you: *correlation does not equal causation.* In business, we too frequently use data to support an existing viewpoint of what works, and not to challenge it.

Secondly, the teachers were so convinced they were right, they had not sought to independently verify if they were correct.[17] There was no incentive for them to challenge this received wisdom. Most of us would probably have done the same, and believed that praise and criticism work in this way.

It was only by independently verifying this through experimentation that they found it was a false assumption. If a business does not value the scientific method, then its understanding of what really influences behaviour will always be limited – because why challenge what you intuitively think works?

Kahneman later wrote: "it is part of the human condition that we are statistically punished for rewarding others and rewarded for punishing them."[18] It is only if you accept that it is also part of the human condition that we make these systemic, system-1-led errors, and are frequently flawed decision-makers as a result, that you arrive at the often counter-intuitive insights and solutions that deliver business success.

Thirdly, what the teachers reported was happening was not what was actually happening. Because a greater proportion of our actions than we realise are subject to the unconscious heuristics and biases studied by behavioural scientists (i.e. we are Homer more often than we think), simply taking at face value what people say about their behaviour only gives you part of the answer. Or, as in this case, a completely wrong one – because they were focusing on one isolated data point, which was not representative. They were concerned with the output of this process (the next flight), not the overall desired outcome (delivering a consistently successful pilot).

The Israeli Air Force subsequently changed its approach to assessing and feeding back on performance as a result of this research – no longer reviewing based on isolated incidents and biased perceptions, and providing feedback accordingly.

---

17   An example of confirmation bias, explained on page 143.
18   *The Undoing Project.*

If, as a business, you want to get to the truth about behaviour, you need to look at the data based on observed, actual (and not claimed) behaviour over time. And focusing on accurate measures of actual behaviour – rather than other metrics that focus on attitudes, awareness, or opinion – is the only way to truly become a behavioural business.

In the remainder of this part, we will look at what we can learn from this approach to build a behavioural business – and how the correct use of observable data on actual (not claimed) behaviour, via the scientific method, can give a competitive advantage. But first, we shall look at what we can learn from how governments have been applying science to change behaviour.

CHAPTER 2

Nudging For Good –
How Governments Use
Behavioural Science

How to change an irrational
behaviour: smoking

T O DEMONSTRATE HOW governments have been leading the way in applying behavioural science, let's look at an example of a behaviour successfully addressed using these principles: smoking.

Smoking is the single largest driver of health inequalities in the UK, killing nearly 78,000 people every year in England alone.[19] I spent a large part of my public service career addressing this challenge. In 2006, I first joined the public sector as a campaigns manager at the Department of Health, and my role was delivering public information campaigns designed to encourage people to quit.

Smoking is in many ways the quintessential, irrational behaviour. Spock would never touch a cigarette. The legacy of consistent government campaigning for over 40 years means virtually all smokers know it is bad for them. Most want to quit. But lack of willpower, plus the chemically addictive and habit-forming nature of smoking, means they find it hard to do so. Focusing on rational drivers of behaviour – simply providing the logical reasons for quitting – was not going to achieve our campaign objective to reduce overall adult smoking rates to 21% or less by 2010.

---

19 NHS England, Statistics on Smoking – England, 2018.

All of our work was couched in terms of behaviour. Everything we did was assessed on the basis of whether it was likely to influence people to quit smoking, and stay that way. The metrics for policy and campaigns were mostly in terms of smoking-related behaviour – overall smoking rates, people attending NHS Stop Smoking Services, and calling our helpline or visiting our website.

Much of the evidence of efficacy was based on flawed data – on what smokers were telling us, which was not necessarily an accurate reflection of what was driving their behaviour, as we will see in part five. The principles we were applying were from social marketing, or how to use established marketing techniques to change behaviour for good. Much of the theory that informed this was based on psychology, and understanding the irrationalities of human behaviour.

To build a new departmental tobacco marketing strategy, our team worked with an external strategist, the leading ad planner Kate Waters, now director of client strategy and planning at the UK broadcaster, ITV.

As Waters put it when I interviewed her in early 2019 at Now, the advertising agency she co-founded: "I did a psychology degree and I never imagined that it would be particularly relevant or useful – in fact I think I managed to forget most of it – until about ten years later when I was working on a brief from the British Heart Foundation, where I had a hunch that psychology might be useful. It was an amazing brief which was essentially 'the government wants to get more people to stop smoking, and think we should scare people into doing so, but they are concerned that the NHS as a brand is too nice and caring and sharing to do that.' So they asked the British Heart Foundation to think about what we could do to add another voice to the debate around tobacco control.

"The ad that resulted is what became known as the fatty cigarette campaign, which I think was probably the most disgusting ad – and I mean that quite literally, as in to elicit disgust – that TV had seen for some time. Possibly ever.

"Smokers have a very deep relationship with the act of smoking, but interestingly they have a slightly more ambivalent relationship with the cigarette itself, and we wanted to turn the venom on the cigarette. We wanted to get to the point where smokers had a 'Pavlovian' response so whenever they saw a cigarette they couldn't help but think of the gunk collecting in their arteries."

Several years later, this was still the most recalled campaign amongst smokers. More than 14,000 people gave up smoking as a direct result of the campaign.[20]

Every cigarette we smoke makes fatty deposits stick in our arteries.

We'll help you give up before you clog up completely. bhf.org.uk

Source: BHF Fatty Cigarettes Campaign Ad, 2004[21]

When Waters compiled our department's marketing strategy a few years later, she brought in insights like this from behavioural science to help people quit more successfully. The strategy changed from simply giving people rational reasons to quit based on the long-term consequences of smoking (e.g. increased risks of heart disease, stroke, and lung cancer), to more emotive and immediate short-term effects that leverage heuristics and biases, as in this example.[22] Additionally, the campaign put equal focus (and budget) on providing tools to help people stay smoke-free, after the initial attempt to quit. These included a number of psychologically informed nudges at relevant times to boost quitters' motivation and willpower, delivered by text messages and email, including positive messages about the health benefits that non-smokers experience.

---

20 www.thirdsector.co.uk/change-makers-british-heart-foundation/communications/article/1192942
21 If you are curious, Waters told me that the 'fat' in the cigarette was made using a combination of hummus and wallpaper paste. Which must have smelt disgusting.
22 In part five we shall see that the motivational messaging subsequently centred on the consequences of smoking on smokers' families.

This worked spectacularly. Over 100,000 people responded to our 2008 campaign to seek NHS help to quit, and we delivered the 21% target by 2009 – a year early. And it personally inspired me to start applying these principles more regularly in my work, in both the public and private sectors.

Nudging for good

A few months later in 2008, the book *Nudge* was published. Written by Cass Sunstein, a Harvard law professor, and Richard Thaler, a University of Chicago economics professor, this showed how insights from behavioural economics could be used to encourage better behaviours, through 'nudging' or 'libertarian paternalism'.

Few books have had such a widespread impact on the practices of governments and beyond. The premise is relatively simple. Using their Spock and Homer analogy, Thaler and Sunstein demonstrated the most effective way to change behaviour is often to 'nudge' our desired behaviours – eating better, saving for retirement, donating our organs – because we lack the ability or willpower to achieve this due to our innate biases.

Rational appeals to our system-2 processes will be ineffective in those situations. In the smoking example, a smoker's Spock brain knows it is better for them to quit – but Homer stops them doing it.

They define a nudge as a subtle, often seemingly insignificant, change to the 'choice architecture' – the way a choice is presented – which influences the choice taken. The numbers of people registered as organ donors, for example, can be significantly increased by moving to an 'opt-out', not 'opt-in', model, i.e. everyone is assumed to consent to be an organ donor unless they explicitly say otherwise, typically when completing a government form.[23] Similarly, putting healthy food on more accessible (e.g. lower)

---

23 However, this does not necessarily increase the number of people who receive organ donations. The issue is a complex one, as it is also heavily determined by the processes employed by hospitals when a donor dies – as they need to then obtain consent by the next of kin, and have the right staff and logistics in place to ensure the organ can be received and transported in time to be used by the donor. The single biggest improvement in live organ donation success rates in the UK was actually achieved by having a dedicated donor nurse active in each NHS hospital. Obviously having more people on the register is helpful to increase the pool of donors, but the debate is whether a mandated opt-in (so that everyone has to state their preference, and let their next of kin know their intention) is preferable to an opt-out system, which leaves potential doubt about their wishes in the event of their death, and so leads to more next-of-kin refusals. Scotland and Wales have moved to an opt-out system in recent years, and at time of writing England has stated an intention to do the same.

shelves in a supermarket increases the number of people buying those products rather than unhealthy snacks.

The visceral warnings on cigarette packs also qualify as a nudge, because they do not restrict the ability to buy cigarettes, but instead make it more cognitively difficult to buy (less attractive). Similarly, making cigarettes more physically difficult to buy (putting them in an unmarked locked cabinet, for example) is another nudge.

The approach gained instant favour among government policy-makers. The advantages are clear: firstly, it does not force citizens to change behaviour, as their ability to choose is maintained and their individual liberty is upheld; secondly, changes to choice architecture are typically low-cost, low-impact interventions; and thirdly, by 'going with the grain' of peoples' desired behaviour, nudges are unlikely to cause widespread objection or unrest among citizens.

As we will explore throughout this book, these are also significant benefits to business. If nudging behaviour is easier, cheaper and reflects sentiment towards the business and brand, then, by definition, it is a more profitable approach than the alternatives. That is, a shove (forcing people into a particular action, such as removing a product from sale) or what Sunstein calls a 'sludge' (making it harder for people to achieve a desired outcome, such as making it difficult to unsubscribe from a service).

Behavioural government

In 2009, the Cabinet Office produced a report with The Institute for Government called 'MINDSPACE', which sought to guide policy-makers on how to use these principles. Sunstein became a key advisor to the Obama administration, and Thaler was integral to the establishment of the Behavioural Insights Team (BIT) – the new 'nudge unit' strategy team created under David Cameron's government in 2010, led by David Halpern (one of the authors of 'MINDSPACE').

A number of the founding personnel and principles for the BIT were from the Behaviour Change Unit previously established at the COI, the centralised government marketing department where I was working as a communications planner at the time.[24] Using these insights from

---

24 The now defunct COI (Central Office of Information) was established shortly after the Second World War, as the successor to the Ministry of Information (the propaganda

behavioural economics, social marketing and social psychology, the COI had also produced a report in 2009 on best practice communications and behaviour change. With my colleague, Guy Dominy, we designed a training program for government communicators based on principles from this and 'MINDSPACE' – drawing on examples from the tobacco campaign, in particular, to illustrate how a focus on nonconscious influences can successfully drive behaviour change.

From here, the BIT has grown to have a presence in five countries globally, and the model has been adopted in a widespread fashion elsewhere, with the creation of numerous 'nudge units'. This growth has been driven by a scientific application of the findings of behavioural science.

In government, where accountability is paramount, this evidence-based approached has proven revolutionary. As Halpern puts it: "This is just a glimpse of an exciting and important future: where policy and practice is based on hard evidence, not just instinct or history, and where public money can go further and outcomes continually improved."[25]

Guided by successes such as the reduction in smoking prevalence, governments have moved from a narrow application of the insights from behavioural science in (social) marketing to a much broader, scientific, outcome-based application. There is much that business can learn from this approach.

Nudging through technology: My QuitBuddy

In 2012, I moved to Australia to take up a role as strategy director at the media agency (UM) for the Australian Federal Government.

---

department), initially to inform the nation about the newly created NHS. It is perhaps best known for producing much-loved public information films such as 'Charlie Says' and 'The Spirit of Dark Water', as well as for well-respected evidence-based best practice in behaviour change communications. Despite its integral role in the creation of the BIT, it was closed by Cameron's government in 2012 as part of austerity measures. Following a public vote of no confidence in its successor by the Institute of Practitioners in Advertising (due to its procurement processes), a new Government Communications Service was subsequently established – effectively a COI 2.0. Meanwhile, nearly all COI staff had either left (like me), taken redundancy, or moved on to other departments.

25 www.theguardian.com/public-leaders-network/small-business-blog/2014/feb/03/nudge-unit-quiet-revolution-evidence

As in the UK, smoking was the single biggest preventable cause of death in Australia. And despite a long heritage of effective behaviour change campaigns giving Australia one of the lowest smoking rates in the developed world, smokers continued to smoke despite being aware of the risks. It was clear, as in the UK, that focusing on the desired behavioural outcome (getting people to quit and stay quit) would be more effective at reducing smoking rates than simply giving rational reasons to give up – giving them the how, rather than telling them why. It would also be considerably more efficient (i.e. cheaper) than an expensive advertising campaign – an example of what Thaler calls "making it easy", his three-word summary of *Nudge*.

When I joined, my new colleagues at UM had talked to our government clients about using then-new mobile app technology to help people quit. Bringing insights into effective ways of nudging behaviour – such as the importance of social proof (i.e. seeing that others had successfully quit using the app) and saliency (i.e. providing bespoke information to each user) – we built an app with development partners The Project Factory called My QuitBuddy.

The first version was built in a mere eight weeks and was very much based on an MVP (Minimum Viable Product) approach,[26] with fairly limited functionality. It included motivational messages of support, a game that smokers could use to distract themselves when experiencing cravings, the ability to record motivational messages from loved ones and provided up-to-date data each time a smoker opened the app on how much money they had saved, toxic tar they had avoided and so on.

After launch, My QuitBuddy quickly achieved the number-one ranking in the Health and Fitness category on the iOS app store, with over 100,000 downloads in the first year. Seven years on, it is still going strong. It has been downloaded over half a million times, and the quitting success rate of users is eight times higher than smokers without support. The app has been white-labelled for use by a number of other governments and is still a key part of Australian government stop-smoking campaigns. It is probably the most effective stop-smoking intervention employed to date by the Federal Government.

---

26 This was mainly because the minister for health wanted a major announcement she could make on World No Tobacco Day on 31 May 2012 – which was eight weeks away. Whilst it was a stretch to make this target, it was the right thing to do in hindsight. The minister had an eight-minute slot on primetime TV programme *The Project* (the Australian version of *The One Show*) where she talked about the app for most of that running time. This PR exposure was hugely effective at driving downloads, which snowballed from there.

Why has it proven so successful? The initial insight behind developing an app was that most quit attempts fail because cravings can hit at any time, so timely support needs to be within arm's reach at any moment. For most of us, the only thing within arm's reach 24 hours a day is our mobile phone. The technological solution was therefore built around an insight into the desired behaviour – and not created for its own sake.

But, more importantly, we were able to create a more effective, addictive and usable app because we had data on what parts of the app people were using. It has been continually updated over the last seven years based on data on actual behaviour.

For example, we found app users were screen-grabbing the homepage (which showed how much money they had saved, how long they had been smoke-free, etc.) and posting it to social media accounts. In the spirit of making it easy, we updated the app to allow users to directly link it to their Facebook and Twitter accounts, so that with one tap they could post an update. This leveraged two behavioural biases: commitment bias (making a public commitment makes us more likely to stick to a behaviour, in this case telling all your friends you have quit); and social proof (showing how popular the app was would encourage others to download and use it).[27]

The app was continually optimised based on actual user data and behavioural science best practice, a distinct advantage over a traditional, one-hit advertising campaign.

I think this example of how behavioural science has been used to address an important societal problem can tell us a lot about how to solve business problems, as well as save lives, and has been hugely informative in my own work. It tells us about the importance of focusing on (behavioural) outcomes, like helping people quit rather than simply telling them why they should. Similarly, it shows us how behavioural science can lead to a better evidence base and enable more creative solutions (such as the fatty cigarette campaign), as well as how technological solutions work best when grounded in a behavioural insight, rather than simply a desire for novelty or innovation. We shall explore this more in part two.

In the next chapter, we will see how this kind of scientific approach – based on testing, learning and optimising – is fundamental to building a successful behavioural business.

---

27 See page 10 for an explanation of social proof.

CHAPTER 3
Test-Tube Behaviours – How to Deliver Marginal Gains Using Behavioural Science

'Sciencing the shit' out of problems

I N THE OSCAR-NOMINATED movie *The Martian*, Matt Damon plays a NASA botanist stuck on Mars. His crew have departed after they have (reasonably) assumed he has been killed by an accident during their mission.

Damon's character survives. It will be several years before a rescue mission can reach him – but he only has sufficient supplies to last a few months. As a highly qualified scientist, he does not panic. He decides to solve the problem in the most effective way possible.

In his words, he decides to "science the shit" out of the problem.

He consults the notes left behind by his colleagues, experiments using the limited resources at his disposal – including a highly creative way of growing potatoes with the help of his own faeces – and he keeps himself alive.

Not only is this a great movie, but it is also a powerful allegory for the way science has solved mankind's problems. The houses we live in, the food we eat, the transport we use: all of these contain innovations that were developed by scientists using the scientific method.

A hypothesis based on existing evidence, followed by a deduction, and tested through observation. Then repeat.

And yet, in business, little work is scientifically based. In fact, most of it involves no experimentation and an awful lot is based on outdated assumptions. Isn't it time we removed the guesswork?

One of the characteristics of governmental behavioural teams like the BIT is their use of best practice, scientific methods. Often, this means using randomised controlled trials (RCTs). David Halpern, CEO of the BIT, calls them the "gold standard of evidence-based policy".[28]

RCTs are a methodology developed by medical science, where the efficacy of a medicine (for example) is tested by evaluating that medicine against a control condition, that is, one where no medicine (or an existing medicine or placebo) is given. Patients are allocated at random (hence the name), with the aim of eliminating bias. Data is then analysed to look for statistically significant differences between the two groups' outcomes to determine not only effectiveness, but also potential side effects.

Social (including behavioural) science experiments generally involve testing a behavioural intervention (nudge) against a control condition – which is usually no change. In one BIT tax experiment for HM Revenue and Customs, they tested a social proof letter saying, "Most people pay their tax on time". This was then evaluated against the existing HMRC letter, with taxpayers receiving one of the two letters at random. The test letter resulted in a 15% increase in the number of people paying before the deadline.

Having seen the overall success of this new letter in getting people to pay their tax on time, the BIT team interrogated the data a bit further. They found that amongst the top 5% of taxpayers, the social proof message had actually *reduced* the likelihood of paying on time by 25%.[29]

Amongst this group – it failed.

To find out what did work for this group, the BIT ran another RCT in 2015 to see what message worked best amongst the highest taxpayers. This turned out to be a loss aversion[30] message based on the effect on public

---

28 www.theguardian.com/public-leaders-network/small-business-blog/2014/feb/03/nudge-unit-quiet-revolution-evidence
29 Halpern hypothesised that this is due to large taxpaying businesses viewing themselves as unique, and so what other people do (the essence of social proof) was viewed as irrelevant.
30 Explained overleaf.

services of not paying tax – this increased payment rates by 8% amongst the highest taxpayers.

And, thus, progress was made. Hypothesis, deduction, observation.

Or, to put it another way: test, learn, adapt. In this case, it was only possible to understand how behaviour was heavily influenced by this context (i.e. the choice architecture) by sciencing the shit out of the problem.

LOSS AVERSION

You may have experienced FOMO (fear of missing out), or the realisation that you want to do something (e.g. going to a party or seeing a movie) not because you especially desire it, but because you fear regretting not doing so. This is a manifestation of a particularly prevalent behavioural bias: loss aversion.

Put simply, loss aversion is the tendency for our behaviour to be more influenced by the risk of a negative outcome (loss), than the chance of gain. We generally feel the loss of £5 more keenly than gaining £5. It explains related biases like the endowment effect (that we value something we own more highly than an identical item we don't) and scarcity bias (our increased desire for things we think are in short supply).

Evolutionary psychologists explain this in terms of our survival instincts. In a world of scarce resources, we needed to ensure that we harness and keep as much as we can, while we can, for fear it might be gone tomorrow. Even in a world of relative abundance, this still guides our behaviour.

Consequently, we also have a present bias: we value things more today than in the future, largely because we can better visualise what we can do with resources (e.g. money) now. It explains why we are generally so bad at saving for retirement, and often reach the end of the month with less money in the bank than we expected.

This bias is used frequently by businesses, particularly in marketing, through limited time offers, closing down sales and the like. In the digital world, when buying tickets or hotel rooms, for example, we often see it through nudges like 'only 5 left at this price!' Instinctively, this makes us want the product more and we become more likely to purchase immediately. But, note the clever phrasing here: 'at this price', means the price could just as well go down as up! Our inherent bias makes us assume that if we don't grab it now, it will cost us.

When working with the call centre described later in this chapter, we experimented with using loss aversion for customer benefit. When talking about the benefits of moving to online banking – specifically that it is safer, quicker, and better for the environment (because it removes the need to send out paper statements) – we found we could significantly increase the likelihood of customers taking up the service by simply suggesting that if they didn't, they would miss out. Previously, customer service representatives (CSRs) had quite rationally talked through these benefits, but found customers tended to ignore the information or cut them off before they finished.

Simply saying that a customer would miss out by not changing worked much better – often without the need to even say what the benefits are (suggesting they already knew what they were, they were just too cognitively lazy/uninterested to change). If a customer queried this, the CSR could then talk them through the advantages, but, in most cases, the decision had already been made.

This is yet another example of how much faster our instinctive system-1 processes are than our more conscious system-2 ones – and more influential.

Learning from failure

In his book *Black Box Thinking*, the journalist Matthew Syed contrasts two industries – medicine and aviation – in terms of how they encourage best practice and avoid the negative outcomes of failure (which is often death). In contrast to how medicines are tested using RCTs, he found that the medical industry does not generally adopt a scientific approach in its response to failure. Medical mistakes are often covered up, ignored, or worse – usually for fear of reprisal and legal action.

But as Syed puts it: "science [is] a discipline where learning from failure is part of the method." This is why the introduction of black boxes in the 1960s – that retain all data pertinent to an air crash (which is then shared globally amongst the entire industry)[31] – has had such an impact on aviation safety.

Indeed, 2017 was the first year on record where there was not a single fatality as a result of a commercial airline crash. A total of 399 people died globally solely in freight and military crashes that year – by contrast, in 1972, a total of 3,346 people were killed.[32]

Syed categorises this scientific approach to failure as characteristic of a 'growth mindset' (as opposed to a 'fixed mindset') for organisations, and the best way to deliver incremental improvements through marginal gains. He quotes the philosopher and scientist Karl Popper: "The history of science, like the history of all human ideas, is a history of ... error. But science is one of the very few human activities – perhaps the only one – in which errors are systematically criticised and fairly often, in time, corrected. This is why we can say that, in science, we learn from our mistakes and why we can speak clearly and sensibly about making progress."

If a business wishes to progress, grow and succeed, then understanding the merits of a scientific approach, and the value of testing, is critical. It must also recognise that this process is an iterative one, where we can learn as much from failure as from success, as with the BIT HMRC experiment. In this way, behavioural science – by requiring testing to establish what works in a realistic context – can increase the effectiveness of established management techniques based on continuous improvement and marginal gains, such as kaizen, lean thinking, and agile processes.

Applying a growth mindset to business challenges

As an example of this, in 2017/8 I worked on a project with partners at OEE Consulting,[33] a leading services and operations management consultancy. The client was an outsourcer that ran a call centre for one of the UK's largest savings banks (having over 20 million customers). OEE Consulting

---

31 This is agreed by international treaty.
32 Data from the Bureau of Aircraft Accidents Archives (B3A), a non-government organisation based in Geneva. Worth noting also that the volume of air traffic (i.e. the number of people carried by air) has increased over that period from 331m annually, to nearly 4bn (International Civil Aviation Organization, Civil Aviation Statistics of the World and ICAO staff estimates).
33 Now GoBeyond Partners.

were developing a number of new processes and systems, based on lean principles, to deliver better processes in the call centre. These had both an efficiency (i.e. money-saving) objective and an effectiveness one (i.e. delivering better service for customers).

I was brought in to advise on how we could deliver better customer service through addressing what customer service representatives (CSRs) were saying on the phone. That is, using behavioural nudges to improve the quality of outcomes for both customers (more successfully answering their reason for calling, such as making a balance transfer) and the bank (reducing the duration of calls so they could handle more, as well as encouraging customers to take up online and paperless offerings).[34]

One example: our analysis found a surprisingly high number of people were failing the mandatory security checks. After listening to calls, we discovered this was because the framing of these checks was very formal, and slightly confrontational. CSRs were in effect saying that if customers could not prove their identity, the bank could (and would) not help. With older customers in particular, this interrogatory approach was causing them undue stress – which has been proven to affect mental availability[35] and the ability to recall information. As a result they would frequently panic and get their answers to the mandatory security questions wrong. This lengthened the call, as well as making it unsuccessful and frustrating for the customer.

With a few small tweaks to the wording, we changed the scripts to frame them more positively (e.g. from "if you prove your identity" to "when you prove your identity")[36] and even said to customers that they could "take their time", to put them more at ease – a counter-intuitive solution. By slowing down the conversation, this would actually *reduce* the overall length of the call.

It is an example of how behavioural science tells us that *how* you say something is as important as *what* you are saying – if not more so.

This was one of multiple interventions (nudges) employed. For practical reasons it was not possible to run a full RCT to isolate each nudge. Instead

---

34   In line with Thaler and Sunstein's objective of going with the grain of behaviour, there is a win-win situation here in that no one likes spending more time on the phone to the bank than necessary, so successfully achieving the objective of the call more quickly benefits both parties. Call duration inversely correlated to customer satisfaction.

35   See the description of availability bias on page 14.

36   This uses the concept of self-efficacy, the behavioural bias that our own belief in our ability to achieve an outcome affects the likelihood of that outcome, to make the customer more likely to successfully complete security.

we ran a controlled pilot where a representative sample of CSRs in the call centre were trained and coached in using these nudges over a 12-week period, and we monitored the outcome of those calls versus the rest of the call centre.

Referring back to our three criteria for a behavioural business from chapter 1: we were using data to build an accurate picture of what worked; we verified it through experimentation; and we had hard data on what was actually happening through data based on behavioural outcomes (the outcome of the phone call). There was a clear, direct link between what our decisions were as a business, and a behavioural outcome.

Over the course of the pilot, there was an 11% reduction in the duration of calls versus the control,[37] worth potentially millions of pounds due to the thousands of calls handled every day. Customer satisfaction levels increased, and we could prove overall success in terms of efficiency and effectiveness based on behavioural outcomes. Subsequently the training and process was rolled out to the other 300 CSRs in the call centre.

The value of testing

But, you may be thinking, for my business to make best practice use of insights from behavioural science, does this mean I need to be conducting RCTs every time I want to nudge a behaviour? Do I need a team of behavioural science PhDs conducting longitudinal, statistical analysis on the most effective subject line before I send an email?

Well, as in the example above, experience says no. RCTs are not the only way to experiment, and in the world of business they are often not practical for reasons of time or money. Besides, in the real world, human behaviour is complex. With over 200 different behavioural biases identified in research, the sheer number of influences on our behaviour often make it impossible to isolate the impact of individual nudges.

Richard Shotton, author of *The Choice Factory* and expert in applied behavioural science in marketing, says the most important thing for experimentation is creating a realistic context, not just sample size. "Context is hugely important, and hugely under-estimated," he says. "The

---

37 The effect was actually greater in relative terms as the rest of the call centre experienced an increase in call duration over the course of the pilot, for various operational reasons.

two reasons for testing are for persuasion and proof, using observed and not claimed data."

For example, I have seen the exact same phrasing used in scripting for two different call centres achieve two entirely different outcomes. But this simply emphasises the importance of testing in the relevant context. In the example above, had we simply applied the academic principles blindly without piloting first it would have been an unacceptable business risk – and completely unscientific.

Leigh Caldwell, co-founder of The Irrational Agency and author of *The Psychology of Price*, agrees. "You never know for sure what's going to work until you test in the field," he says. "Everyone is influenced by context, because everyone has their own view of the world."

Even Richard Thaler himself says: "Make your research about the world, not the literature."[38]

The difference is that in business, what we do is not subject to peer review, nor do we publish our experiments in academic journals. That would wholly undermine any competitive advantage. As Rory Sutherland,[39] author of *Alchemy: The Surprising Power of Ideas That Don't Make Sense*, vice-chairman of Ogilvy UK, and the foremost advocate of behavioural science in marketing, puts it: "Let me briefly explain what business and behavioural science have in common. They both do experiments. Apart from that, everything is slightly different."[40]

Businesses seek competitive advantage above all else, and, as we have seen, a scientific approach to changing behaviour can drive progress and innovation to deliver that. Whether that is achieved by academically robust experimentation, or simply adopting a mindset of continuous testing and learning, hypothesising and deducing, is largely irrelevant. This also means businesses should not be unduly concerned about the current academic debate about whether certain experimental psychological studies can be reproduced – the so-called replication crisis. Especially when one considers the replication rate of social psychology experiments actually compares favourably with medical disciplines, like oncology.

As Sutherland states: "In science, the dream is to uncover a universal, timeless truth or law. In business, we don't need to be right in general – we just need to make the best decision for the situation at hand ... In business,

---

38 On Twitter, when asked to give his most important advice to PhD students.
39 Also, in the interests of full disclosure, my former boss.
40 behavioralscientist.org/it-isnt-a-replication-crisis-its-a-replication-opportunity

you don't need to be 'right'. You just need to be right enough ... Sometimes all you need is to be less wrong than your competitors."

Or, to put it another way, a business can science the shit out of a problem without needing a PhD. But a business also has to become comfortable with the fact that some of the results may not always be what you expect.

In fact, because behavioural science is grounded in understanding the nonconscious, hidden drivers of behaviour, they almost certainly will not be as expected. Sutherland says this is an inherent (competitive) advantage.

"Every time you test these things you find significant events – not necessarily predictably. But they're significant enough at the very least to be worth testing. And the gains are monumental ... I think there's a massive sweet spot, because people only test what's rational. The burden of proof we apply to a rational suggestion is very low. And the burden of proof we apply to an irrational suggestion is very, very high.

"But actually irrational suggestions, if they succeed, are much more valuable, because it's knowledge you have which might give you one up over your competitors. That is a really valuable insight, whereas merely confirming what you already know is almost worthless."

The conclusion is clear. "Test counter-intuitive things," he advocates. "Because your competitors won't."

The value of this has been, in my experience, that the budgetary commitments are also much less. Should you hire a traditional management consultancy like McKinsey, for example, to address a problem they may spend hundreds of thousands of pounds developing a report of several hundred pages, that advocates one solution.

Hire a behavioural scientist and you will likely get a ten-page report with ten solutions that you can practically test to prove what works. Behavioural science solutions are as open to small businesses and start-ups as they are to large corporates – and can level the playing field.

McKinsey themselves even acknowledged this critical role in their 2019 review of behavioural science in the corporate world: "Creating an effective nudge unit requires much more than hiring a few experts who understand heuristics and statistics. It's up to senior management to create the conditions for success by helping to focus the unit, situate it in the organization, celebrate its impact, and hold it to high ethical standards."[41]

---

41 'Lessons from the front line of corporate nudging', *McKinsey Quarterly*, January 2019.

My interviews with leading behavioural practitioners confirmed they have found great value in an experimental approach – what I like to call 'test-tube behaviours'.

David Perrott, an established South African practitioner, says an experimental approach actually fosters creativity, rather than the opposite: "Experimentation allows for more creativity, more counter-intuitiveness and innovative techniques, because it is viewed as a test. Because no one's neck is on the line if it fails."

In the following parts of the book, we will explore how an understanding of behavioural science, and applying test-tube behaviours, can lead to benefits in key areas of business, and how some leading businesses have effectively applied this knowledge.

Next we will see how removing this stigma of failure through a growth mindset, and an experimental approach to understanding the drivers of human behaviour, has driven the growth of the most successful global businesses in the 21st century. In addition, we will see how it is baked into the culture of these organisations.

CHAPTER 4

How to Create a Behavioural Business

WHAT TO DO NOW

I N THIS PART, we have seen how behavioural science demonstrates that:

- much of human decision-making is more emotional, less rational, and more instinctive than we assume;

- as a consequence, much of our behaviour is heavily influenced by context and our innate biases and heuristics;

- changing that context (the choice architecture) even in very small ways can have a significant impact on behaviour;

- a scientific, evidence-based approach to applying behavioural science has helped governments address a number of important issues, such as smoking;

- to determine the most effective ways to change behaviour, it is important to test, in as close to the real-world context as possible, and collect data on actual (not claimed) behaviour;

- to effectively do this in business requires a growth mindset, i.e. recognising that we can learn as much from failure as from success;

- for businesses, doing this has been proven to generate marginal gains (in terms of both efficiency and effectiveness) and achieve competitive advantage.

Consequently, there are a number of things you can do to make effective use of the science to become a behavioural business:

- ensure you understand that people are most often in Homer mode, i.e. will not think unless they have to, and so create processes, systems, products and services that make it easy to achieve a desired behaviour;

- focus on collecting data on actual, not claimed, behaviour based on the desired outcomes;

- make hypotheses based on data and create infrastructure to conduct experiments to verify them, i.e. science the shit out of problems;

- encourage *test-tube behaviours* – promote continuous testing and learning, building of new hypotheses, and testing creative, counter-intuitive solutions;

- be prepared that some of these experiments may fail, and that learning from these failures is an important part of a growth mindset that delivers marginal gains in both efficiency, and effectiveness.

PART
TWO

Delivering in Digital with Behavioural Science

CHAPTER 5

How Digital Got its FANGs – the Behavioural Science of Digital Business

'Making it easy' in digital

T HE LARGEST GLOBAL digital companies – the so-called FANG group (Facebook, Amazon, Netflix, Google) – are worth a combined total of over $2,350 billion at the time of writing. But none were the first to launch in their respective markets, nor was the technology they employed unique. They did not deliver that growth solely through technical innovation.

In differing ways, every FANG company demonstrates how creating processes, systems, products and services that make it easy – by paying close attention to the psychology of customers – leads to business success.

And yet, providers of digital goods and services often seem to forget (or ignore) that consumers frequently want their decisions – and therefore their lives – made easy for them. That the digital customer experience should be short, not long, and require as little effort on their part as possible. And not just minimal physical effort, like next-day home delivery, but *mental* effort as well.

The most successful digital companies of the 21st century have minimised consumer cognitive effort. The FANGs have achieved market dominance in social, e-commerce, content and search by providing products that are not just driven by technological innovation, but go with the grain of behaviour, reduce friction, and make choice as easy as possible. They leverage instinctive system-1 biases and heuristics to provide experiences that are effortless, turning them into habits and making their products inherently addictive – with all the associated ethical and moral problems that causes, as we shall see later.

Let's take a quick example. Do you remember the heady days of 1998? When the biggest Presidential scandal involved an act of infidelity with an intern, European countries agreed to work more closely and introduce a single currency, and Britney Spears informed us that, oops, she had done it again?

On 28 September of that year, a shiny new search engine called Google launched.

Google was not the first search engine. It wasn't even among the first 50. In 1998, there were dozens of similar products available, including Yahoo!, Altavista, AOL, and Ask Jeeves.[42] Yet, two Stanford dropouts, Sergey Brin and Larry Page, were still able to create a disruptive product, and one that quickly achieved a near monopoly.

Twenty years on, 85% of all internet searches in the UK are conducted using Google. It has been an astonishing rise, with virtually none of that growth fuelled by marketing. Most of Google's marketing efforts have been focused on its other products, such as phones and voice assistants.

Google's innovation in the search market was not technological – their background tech was essentially the same as the other search companies – but *psychological*. The information Google provided was the same as other providers, but the way it was presented to users was different. What they were saying was the same, but how they said it was better. According to Nir Eyal, in his excellent book *Hooked*:

> "Google's PageRank[43] algorithm proved to be a much more effective way to index the web. By ranking pages based on how frequently other sites linked to them, Google improved search relevancy. Compared with directory-based search tools such as Yahoo!, Google was a massive

---

42   Even in 2002, after three very successful years, Google's future dominance was proving hard to predict. A *New York Times* article from that year (following Eric Schmidt's appointment as CEO) said: "…the bigger question is whether Google has the scale to capture a viable share of the search advertising market. In other words, can Google create a business model even remotely as good as its technology?" www.nytimes.com/2002/04/08/business/google-s-toughest-search-is-for-a-business-model.html

43   So named not because it is a ranking of pages, but after Google co-founder Larry Page, fact fans. Something I only learnt myself in writing this.

time-saver. Google also beat out other search engines that had become polluted with irrelevant content and cluttered with advertising. From its inception, Google's clean, simple homepage and search results pages were *solely focused on streamlining the act of searching and getting relevant results.*

"Simply put, Google reduced the amount of time and the *cognitive effort* required to find what the user was looking for."[44]

Leaving aside the pitfall of survivorship bias (see below), this is a great example of how the digital behemoths have been driven by an evidence-based understanding of the psychology of consumers. Through that understanding, they have delivered products and experiences that are more useful, memorable, cognitively effortless and – therefore – more addictive than those of their competitors.

SURVIVORSHIP BIAS

Source: xkcd

---

44 Emphasis added.

The joke in the great cartoon above, of course, is that winning the lottery is down to blind luck. The time put in bears no relation to the chances of winning, but successful people will often post-rationalise success as due to positive character traits.[45]

Hence the expression: "History is written by the victors."

How this biases our behaviour is that we tend to regard stories of success as more influential than unsuccessful ones, and often ignore the effect of chance on positive outcomes.

One famous example of survivorship bias is explained by David McRaney in his book, *You Are Now Less Dumb*. It is the story of Abraham Wald, a statistician working for the Applied Mathematics Panel for the US Air Force during WWII.

The Air Force top brass were concerned about the low survival rates of bomber crews – at one stage they had a 50% chance of surviving a tour of duty. They wanted to increase the chances of crews returning unharmed by reinforcing the armour on the planes. But they couldn't reinforce the plane throughout, because it would make it too heavy to fly and steel was in very short supply.

The military had recorded data on where the returning planes accumulated most bullet holes – along the wings, around the tail gunner, and down the centre of the body – and naturally their first thought was to reinforce those areas.

McRaney explains: "The mistake, which Wald saw instantly, was that the holes showed where the planes were strongest. The holes showed where a bomber could be shot and still survive the flight home, Wald explained. After all, here they were, holes and all. It was the planes that weren't there that needed extra protection, and they had needed it in places that these planes had not."

Wald experimented to determine which of the other areas needed the most protection, saving countless lives. His theories are still in use today.[46]

By only looking at the planes that survived, the US Air Force gained a false picture of what success looked like. This bias blinded them to the fact that there is as much to be learnt from failure (if not more), and negated scepticism about positive outcomes. Accordingly, we

---

45 In this sense, it is a manifestation of the fundamental attribution error, explained on page 173.

46 In an act of supremely tragic irony, Wald and his wife were killed in a plane crash in 1950.

should overcome our natural tendency to hide failures, because if we do not, they are much more likely to be repeated. And we should accept that often our successes happen due to pure good fortune.

This is not only fundamental to a growth mindset, but is also the basis of experimentation. If you test five things in an experiment, and only two work, that isn't a bad outcome, nor a failed experiment.[47] You will have gained five valuable insights that will deliver a business advantage – by doing the things that work, and also by *not* doing the things that don't.

Daniel Kahneman says: "A stupid decision that works out well becomes a brilliant decision in hindsight."

Making search easy: Google

In Google's case, while behavioural insight drove the fundamentals of the product, part of their success was also sheer, dumb luck – it is a fairly open secret that the original Google interface was so clean and simple because Larry Page didn't know how to code in HTML.

Despite this, such was the effectiveness of the approach that the Google homepage remains largely unchanged in 20 years (aside from updated branding and the 'Google doodles'[48]).

---

47 As any scientist will tell you, the only way to deliver a failed experiment is to conduct it in such a way that the outcomes are not robust. In fact, in my work applying behavioural science in business, the 2:3 ratio is fairly typical.
48 Which is a nice example of wholly discretionary (i.e. functionally unnecessary) effort, but which generates a feeling of reciprocity and liking, known as a Kano effect. Colloquially, you might call this going the extra mile. It's the equivalent of the biscuit or chocolate you get with your coffee at a restaurant, or the metal cutlery you get with your meal on a business class flight.

The Google homepage in 1998 (top) and now (bottom)

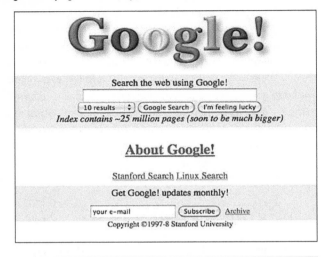

Source: *Hooked* by Eyal, N./Google

One example of how Google makes the experience of searching as cognitively easy as possible is the choice architecture of providing two simple buttons: 'Google Search' and 'I'm Feeling Lucky'.

Have you ever actually used the 'I'm Feeling Lucky' button to conduct your Google search? Me neither. My friends at Google assure me this isn't unusual. A 2007 analysis concluded that fewer than 1% of all search queries are conducted using that button.[49] When users do click it, they go straight to the top result page, skipping the results listings. That means that Google shows zero ads (and therefore gets zero ad clicks) on 1% of all Google search

---

49 www.quora.com/How-many-people-use-the-Google-Im-Feeling-Lucky-search

queries. The analysis concluded that this button costs Google as much as $100m per year in lost ad revenue.[50]

Yet the button still remains. If 'I'm Feeling Lucky' loses Google money when people use it, and hardly anyone uses it anyway, then why is it still there? Nostalgia? The anecdotal feedback from Google insiders is that this placebo choice remains because it subconsciously implies *that Google will always give you the best possible result.*[51]

This subtle nudge, unchanged in 20 years, gives users faith in search results, and increases their self-efficacy (confidence and trust) in the brand to provide the right solution – as with the banking customers and the re-framing of security checks example in chapter 3. It is Google's way of saying that no matter which button you press, it will deliver the result you want. Google is there (it implies) to serve your needs as a user – rather than its advertisers.

Subsequent Google innovations, such as auto-completing queries, spelling corrections and so on, are also based on further improving the cognitive ease of the user experience. This includes using data on your previous search behaviour to make the results you see tailored to you (one change to the homepage since 1998 is the ability to sign in to your Google account). That personalised experience makes it even more effortless, as we like things more if we think they are unique to us.[52] All of which serves to drive our Google addiction, and make it the go-to search engine for 85% of internet users.

Using data to leverage social proof: Netflix

This personalisation effect has also been harnessed by Netflix to achieve market dominance using social proof – our innate desire to follow the herd. They have deployed machine-learning algorithms and customer data

---

50   Nowadays, the button is even less likely to be used due to innovations like 'Google Instant' (search results being displayed as the text is entered) which are more likely to direct users to use listed results – so it is estimated the figure is now much closer to 0%.

51   As we will explore in the next chapter, Google tests *everything* so it is reasonable to assume they have internal evidence to back this up.

52   Based on the concept of saliency, explained on page 14.

to create bespoke experiences for each user – the Netflix pages that you and I see will be different – and also to highlight what other people are doing.

Much has been made of the binge-watching phenomenon, how it has changed the nature of TV viewing, and how specific content makes the site uniquely addictive rather than the site itself. Undoubtedly, if the content on Netflix was solely repeats of 'Allo 'Allo and Heartbeat (like some other channels I can mention), it would not have caught on quite so well with younger TV viewers.

But far more relevant is the fact that more than 80% of all content watched on Netflix is actually based on its recommendation engine. That is, content recommended to a viewer according to a percentage-based ranking, based on things previously watched – effectively a numerical social proof value.

Example of Netflix recommendations

Source: Netflix

No one outside Netflix knows exactly how that percentage matching works (is it based on what other people who liked that also watched? Or who stars in/writes/directs the show? Or genre?).[53] The mechanism for it

---

53   It's supposedly top-secret, but a 2017 Wired article claims it is based on dividing people into 2,000 different 'taste groups' that then allocate recommendations using machine learning algorithms "to help break viewers' preconceived notions and find shows that they might not have initially chosen." www.wired.co.uk/article/how-do-netflixs-algorithms-work-machine-learning-helps-to-predict-what-viewers-will-like

was copied by Netflix from dating sites, which provide matches based on compatibility with other users (such as shared interests).

There is huge potential for this combination of data and behavioural insight to be applied in many other contexts to deliver the most compelling content.

"Netflix are looking at the content itself, the storyline, the characters, a whole range of data points about you and the content," says Steve Thompson, an experienced digital training consultant who works with media businesses across Europe. "And then using that insight to create future content. As a user you will also start to see recommendations down to your consumption of the content. They can easily use machine learning to nudge people into choices about what content they choose in the future."

The net effect is a kind of evolutionary natural selection of content – with only the strongest (i.e. most popular) content surviving, but maintaining sufficient variety to keep us interested. This keeps the content gene pool sufficiently broad – and making the best possible product overall.

Netflix not only personalises recommendations, but *how* they recommend it. The artwork chosen to promote a particular show will be personalised to what is most appealing to each user, featuring different images or actors based on what is most likely to be clicked on.

"We don't have one product but over a 100 million different products," say Netflix. "With one for each of our members with *personalized recommendations* and *personalized visuals.*"[54]

As a result, users implicitly trust the mechanism simply because it takes the pain out of having to choose what to watch. In 2020, the paradox of choice of watching TV is that there is such a huge number of channels and content available it becomes an impossibly hard 'choice-maximisation' problem.

Netflix solves it by providing a simple, 'choice-satisficing' solution: if you liked that, you'll like this. And what do you know? Three out of four times that simple nudge works, along with others, like automatically starting the next episode and the ability to skip the credits, and keeps people watching.

---

54 medium.com/netflix-techblog/artwork-personalization-c589f074ad76

THE PARADOX OF CHOICE

The paradox of choice is a term coined by Professor Barry Schwartz (and the title of his 2004 book). Schwartz's thesis is that in modern, westernised societies, we are now overwhelmed with abundant choice in almost every aspect of modern life: utilities, healthcare, pensions, beauty, work, love, religion, identity. But the paradox is, counter-intuitively, that increasing the choices available does not make us happier, nor make us more likely to choose the option we will like best.

"Autonomy and freedom of choice are critical to our wellbeing, and choice is critical to freedom and autonomy," says Schwartz. "Nonetheless, though modern Americans have more choice than any group of people ever has before, and thus, presumably, more freedom and autonomy, we don't seem to be benefiting from it psychologically."[55]

As an example, Schwartz references a famous experiment by Professor Sheena Iyengar, of Columbia University, and Professor Mark Lepper, of Stanford. In an upmarket San Francisco supermarket they offered customers the chance to sample Wilkin & Son jams, before providing a money-off coupon. Every few hours they switched between offering the chance to sample from a range of six or 24 different jams. Tracking the purchases with the coupon, they found that when participants were faced with the smaller (six) rather than larger (24) array of jam, they were ten times more likely to make a purchase, and were actually more satisfied with their tasting.[56]

Schwartz references Herbert A. Simon's[57] distinction between choice maximising (finding the best possible option when deciding, i.e. perfectionism) and satisficing (choosing a 'good enough' option). The thousands of decisions we make every day mean we cannot maximise in every possible scenario – so many of our decisions are made using simple heuristics to meet our criteria, i.e. become system-1 decisions. Satisficing becomes a practical necessity, but

---

55   *The Paradox of Choice*, Schwartz, B., Harper (2004).
56   The experiment is detailed in Iyengar's book *The Art of Choosing*, Abacus (2010).
57   Nobel Prize winning economist and cognitive psychologist – and therefore with a credible claim to being a founding father of behavioural science.

for decisions that are important, or which turn out badly, this can cause us regret.

Schwartz concludes that the path to happiness in a world of over-abundant choice is to be content with good enough. Recognise the things in life that are important to you personally (or you are an expert in) and focus your decision-making efforts on those. For everything else, the best possible decision may be too difficult, or impossible, and the perfect choice is probably out of reach. Use objective standards rather than subjective ones (e.g. choose your holiday hotel based on TripAdvisor recommendations, rather than where your neighbours went, as this will create more realistic expectations). Besides, everything suffers by comparison. Become a satisficer, not a maximiser, and delegate the unimportant choices where possible.

Creating addictive products: Amazon

The Amazon recommendation engine also leverages social proof by recommending products based on items users have previously purchased:

Example of the Amazon recommendation engine

Source: Amazon

In training that Steve Thompson and I run, we often ask how many people have ever bought based on those recommendations. Usually, one or two hands reluctantly go up. We then tell the group that some of them are probably mistaken – Amazon does not release the data, but it is rumoured that up to 25% of Amazon's revenue is directly driven by the recommendation engine.[58]

Couple that with how Amazon also makes it cognitively easy to use with optimisations like checking out as a guest, one-click ordering, next-day delivery and wish lists (none of which were new tech created by Amazon), and you have a uniquely addictive product. And addictive experiences are critical to the growth of the FANGs. If Amazon still only sold books, it would only have a user base of book readers. Allowing you to buy your shelves, reading lamp and comfy chair from them both increases your profitability as a customer and the pool of Amazon's potential users. But a pool of consumers will only buy from you in meaningful numbers if the experience of buying is a (psychologically) easy one, such that it becomes a system-1 habit – one repeated over and over again.

Building these habits requires creating the right behavioural cues, routines and rewards.[59] Amazon is so confident in its ability to create the habit of purchasing, it actually runs ads for direct competitors on its site. Much like the 'I'm Feeling Lucky' button for Google, this increases trust in its services (as well as generating some extra ad revenue on the side).

For Amazon, making it easy in physical and mental terms creates the habit of being a first port of call for online purchasing – being a "shop for everything" – and is an essential condition for consumers to trust in the brand to deliver the products as purchased, on time and in one piece. Ask Jeeves failed as a search engine because the additional cognitive effort required made it a much worse experience than Google (on Ask Jeeves you had to phrase your search request *as a question!*) even though the results delivered were substantively the same. Similarly, there are literally hundreds of places in the digital and physical world I can buy printer paper, and thereby achieve the same outcome that Amazon delivers. But Amazon is my default, because I can find and purchase the paper I need in a matter of seconds with an absolutely minimal amount of effort – and it already knows exactly where to deliver it.

Amazon has succeeded in making the experience of buying from it cognitively and physically easier than other sites, and therefore more

---

58 As we will explore in part five, it's possible they simply don't remember because they are shopping in automatic mode, and so admittedly this impromptu market research uses a deeply flawed methodology. I met a senior executive from Amazon and asked if he could verify the 25% figure. "I can't confirm that," he replied. "But it is a lot."

59 See the description of the habit loop on page 127.

trusted, because its focus has wholly been on building a product that is based on the best possible experience for the customer. The technology has been built to generate this trust, not the other way round.

This was Amazon CEO Jeff Bezos's ambition from the very beginning, as he stated in a 1999 interview with CNBC: "If there is one thing Amazon is about it is obsessive attention to the customer experience, end to end."

Bezos went on to describe how it is this obsession with the customer, and their needs, that drove the growth of the company – rather than the (then) novelty of being an internet business. "Internet, schminternet," he said. "That doesn't matter. In the long term there is never any mis-alignment between customer interests and shareholder interests."

A famous example, which also shows the importance of testing using actual user data, is Amazon Prime (the paid subscription service that gives customers access to free delivery). Econometric modelling had supposedly shown that the service would be unprofitable – and that proved to be the case in the first year. The behavioural insight behind introducing the service was what Dan Ariely calls 'the power of free' – that is, we place a disproportionately high value on things that we receive for free, and it generates a feeling of reciprocity and favourability towards the givers of the free item.

Longer term, Amazon wanted to see if providing this 'free' service would increase the total spend of those customers, make them more loyal, and therefore more receptive to the new products Amazon would later introduce, such as Video and its Wardrobe clothing service.

In 2018, Bezos confirmed that this "obsessive compulsive focus on the customer as opposed to … the competitor" revealed that Prime had grown to over 100m customers.[60] These customers shop at Amazon on average 25 times a year and spend about $1,300, compared to 14 times and about $700 per year for non-member customers. Interestingly, the data shows they spend no more at each visit, nor buy more items. They just visit more often, and have become more loyal, because Amazon has become their habitual first stop when buying online.[61]

Amazon therefore has tangible evidence that Prime made the product more habit-forming – more addictive.

---

60 www.businessinsider.com/amazon-jeff-bezos-success-customer-obsession-2018-9
61 files.constantcontact.com/150f9af2201/1ade4980-7297-467a-86b5-d6a4b93371e4.pdf

It is a further example of how the FANG companies have achieved global domination by understanding the psychology of users, more than technological innovation. They have created experiences that require the least cognitive effort, are rooted in behavioural science, and are therefore the best possible in psychological terms. These are what gain you millions of customers and keep them coming back.

But how did they arrive at those insights, and what can we learn from the approach? That is what we shall explore in the next chapter.

CHAPTER 6
Digital and the Growth Mindset – the Lean Approach to Using Behavioural Science

W HAT ELSE CAN we learn from the rise of the FANGs? How did they arrive at critical insights into what was driving the behaviour of their users – and use those insights to achieve market dominance?

How did Netflix have the foresight to change its business model into a provider of streaming services[62] (unlike competitors such as Blockbuster), and then deliver an experience that far surpassed other services?

And once Google started generating users as a result of its cognitively easier interface, how did it know the best way to present those results to keep users coming back? And why did Facebook create innovations such as the 'like' button, the news feed, and the ability to tag other users? Similarly, how did Amazon understand the value of recommendations and one-click ordering?

Most importantly, why did they develop these insights, rather than anybody else? And what can we learn about this to allow us to develop better services and experiences for businesses?

Because behavioural science requires us to understand that human behaviour is often irrational, driven by heuristics and biases, and hugely

---

62 Netflix launched in 1997 as a provider of sale and rental DVDs in the post – the US equivalent to LoveFilm in the UK – moving into streaming in 2007.

influenced by the context in which we make decisions, one side effect is that things don't always turn out the way we expect. Which biases are most dominant will vary situation to situation.

Only through experimentation can we establish what will work best. That is why a growth mindset – one that embraces testing, learning, and other test-tube behaviours – is common to all these companies.

Testing using behavioural data

We saw in the previous chapter that the cognitive ease of Google's interface was partly serendipitous, because of Larry Page's limited programming skills. But is this true of the PageRank algorithm too? Did they stumble on this insight about the most effective way to present search results?

"Well, information retrieval was Larry's PhD thesis, so there was a lot of scientific knowledge that went into that," says David Chalmers, an artificial intelligence (AI) consultant and digital product manager, and a Google veteran who spent 11 years as a global product manager for the company in London and Mountain View, California. "But I can guarantee that Google will also have shown the page without the 'Feeling Lucky' button to 1% of users and tested it."

Whether the insight was arrived at by accident, or through a deeper understanding of human behaviour, the behaviours that are intrinsic to Google as an organisation meant they were subsequently verified *scientifically, through experimentation.* What is common among the FANG companies (aside from grounding their innovation in delivering the best experience in psychological terms) is a rigorous, evidence-based approach to developing insights. The test-tube behaviours of using actual, outcome-based data, and a growth mindset approach to delivering marginal gains, are baked into how these companies work.

The shade of blue used to show results in the Google toolbar (for example) is a result of testing over 40 different colours to see what generated the most clicks. This optimisation is estimated to have generated over $200m in additional annual revenue.[63]

As Rory Sutherland says: "Test counter-intuitive things – because your competitors won't."

---

63 *Black Box Thinking*, Syed, M. The figure is quoted by Dan Cobley, Google UK's managing director.

The commonality amongst the most innovative companies is how many experiments they run each year. In 2016 alone, Intuit ran 1,300 experiments, P&G: 7,000–10,000, Google: 7,000, Amazon: 2,000, Netflix: 1,000. Most of these fail but still provide insights for progress – and big wins (what Nicholas Nassim Taleb calls 'black swans') like Amazon Prime more than compensate for the failures.

Actual data on user behaviour is used to test their hypotheses – rather than hunches or best guesses. Every innovation is tested against a subset of their user base to ensure it works before it is delivered to the rest of the world (known as beta testing). By doing this, they remove possible unintended consequences.

"For an A/B test you still need to decide what A and B are," says Chalmers. "If that is baked into your culture, as it is throughout Silicon Valley – as they are following the Google playbook – you change and release things in beta."

And this is one advantage that internet businesses have. They have masses of data on actual, not claimed, behaviour. Amazon knows what you buy, Netflix knows what you watch, Facebook knows who you are friends with, and Google knows what you search for. Not many businesses have access to such rich resources.

They also have the ability to conduct tests and experiments at enormous scale, with thousands of different variations of their sites and apps running at once. Any hypothesis, whether based on behavioural science, a hunch, or some new piece of tech they've spotted on a competitor's site, can be tested scientifically through RCTs.

"The point is, they're willing to experiment," says Chalmers. "And you have the ability to experiment when your product is a website. And the cost of experimentation is low. Once you've embedded that in your culture, the idea of gathering lots of data, and then using those data sets to seek out patterns – which is essentially all machine learning is – just becomes incredibly natural. And, of course, it's helped by the fact that they're stocked up with most of the world's computer science PhDs. It's a bit of a perfect storm. In those Silicon Valley, FANG-oriented companies, there is an inherent advantage. They have the culture, they have the means. And they have a bunch of essentially unfair advantages. Data becomes this valuable commodity."

If your business does not have these inherent, unfair advantages, do not despair – a huge database and a team of PhDs is not essential to embedding test-tube behaviours into your business. Far more important is the willingness to test and learn, and encouraging this amongst your teams. There are also many other more practical, lower-cost ways of generating these insights, which we will explore later in this chapter.

How Facebook embeds test-tube behaviours

Are corporate slogans meaningful? It's easy to be cynical about them. What's interesting about these companies' mantras is that an experimental, evidence-based approach is actually hidden within them, right there in plain sight.

Facebook: "Move fast and break things."

Netflix: "Watch what's next."

Google: "Do the right thing."[64]

Amazon: "Work hard. Have fun. Make history."

With the possible exception of Amazon, they all imply cultures of innovation, testing and evidence-based decision-making. It may not be in the corporate mantra, but Bezos certainly sees it as critical to Amazon's success. He has said: "Our success at Amazon is a function of how many experiments we do per year, per month, per week, per day."[65]

Facebook goes a step further and empowers all its staff to conduct tests, seemingly at will. In an interview with the economist Steven Dubner for the Freakonomics podcast in summer 2017 (notably before the Cambridge Analytica scandal broke), Mark Zuckerberg confirmed that any engineer working for Facebook, wherever they are in the world, has the ability to take the trunk (i.e. standard) version of Facebook and create a new version.

"So one of the basic strategies of our company is to learn as quickly as we can. That is more important to us than any specific strategy of, 'Okay, here's how we're going to build the best messaging app, or here's how we're going to build the best news feed,' is building a company that is just agile and learns as quickly as possible from what people are telling us," he says.

---

64 Famously changed from "Don't Be Evil" in 2014.
65 www.fastcompany.com/3063846/why-these-tech-companies-keep-running-thousands-of-failed

And how do they do this?

"The best way to learn is to basically try things out and get feedback. If you just have one version of Facebook running, that constrains how much people can react to. So we build this whole framework that allows people within the company – any engineer – to change some code, create a new branch of what Facebook is, and ship that to a number of people; maybe 10,000, some small portion of the community in order to get good feedback from that. And there are a bunch of rules around a bunch of things that you can't ship."

One can easily see the advantages, not only in ensuring a growth mindset and continuous innovation, but also in motivating staff. If I was a junior staff member who could point to a key part of the Facebook design and say, "I did that", it would be hugely empowering. As we will explore in part four, feeling powerless or uninfluential is one of the most psychologically debilitating and demotivating aspects of work – the opposite is also true.

There are also very significant risks, which we will explore in the next chapter.

Applying this approach

You may be thinking that your business lacks the inherent advantages of Silicon Valley, and that creating these kind of test-tube behaviours will be difficult, if not impossible. Without the ability to conduct massive RCTs using actual behavioural data, how can you apply these principles and empower people to test, learn and adapt?

In part one, we saw how, for most businesses, the level of rigour required by an RCT is unnecessary. But, as part of a lean approach, we were still able to deliver significant efficiencies in a call centre – some of these came directly as a result of insights from staff. Similarly, the reason that My QuitBuddy remains successful seven years after launch is the minimum viable product approach, pioneered by tech start-ups – that is, building a basic product and then adding functionality and features based on behavioural data from users, and learning in an iterative way.

David Chalmers says: "The most important thing is the culture of continuous improvement. The lean idea that someone in the factory line can stop the line; that as an employee, it's as much my job as the CEO's to improve the process; that is critical. There are some advantages to being a digital company, because maybe it feels easier to have influence – but ultimately, any company can foster that culture. The concept of it being everybody's job to improve process originates in post-war Japan and predates machine learning, artificial intelligence and Silicon Valley."

As an example, in 2018, a credit card provider asked my business to review its website to see whether there were things we could test to behaviourally optimise the site. They had found that, having driven customers to their site, surprisingly few actually went on to apply for a card.

A behavioural audit identified several opportunities to make the user experience cognitively easier – one of which was that users had to scroll through three pages of (largely irrelevant) product information before they even got to the 'apply now' button. For customers in the Homer mindset of simply wanting to get on with the application, this information would require a lot of cognitive effort (system-2 thinking).

Our recommendation was to conduct an A/B test to see how the existing website compared to a version where the button was made more salient – by moving it above the fold, to the top of the web page. The results showed that simply doing this instantly increased the click-through rate to application on the webpage by 54%.

This shows that for businesses that can collect data on actual behaviour and test accordingly, there really are no excuses not to – the benefits are potentially huge. Simply creating a product and expecting people to use it without consideration of nonconscious drivers of behaviour is a recipe for disaster.

It is estimated that 83% of all apps on the App Store are so-called 'zombie apps', with virtually no users.[66] Forrester Research found that most mobile smartphone users spend their time on a mere five non-native (i.e. not pre-installed) apps.[67] I've spoken to, and worked with, multiple start-ups that have created products they perceive to be ground-breakingly innovative, only to be puzzled to find that people stubbornly refuse to use them. They would have saved considerable time and effort by testing some of their hypotheses before embarking on the builds.

I spoke to Paul Armstrong, founder of emerging technology consultancy Here/Forth, tech journalist and author of *Disruptive Technologies; Understand, Evaluate and Respond,* about why so many businesses do not test in this way.

---

66 www.cultofmac.com/310736/zombie-apps-taking-app-store/
67 techcrunch.com/2015/06/22/consumers-spend-85-of-time-on-smartphones-in-apps-but-only-5-apps-see-heavy-use/

"I think so many products nowadays fail the human test," says Armstrong. "I find that people very rarely even consider the human elements until it's either too late or too far baked, and it's hard to retroactively fit ... There's an IP argument that you can't give your idea out too soon or people might steal it. It's never been quicker to be able to make something – or destroy something. I think people just lack the rigour sometimes of having good human testing, because when you get to a certain level, a human could come in and ruin it by saying: 'Why is your handle orange?' There's always that fear...

"But there have never been more tools out there that if you want people's feedback on things, you can get it for free, or less free as I always say, but you can definitely get it. So why we're making so many mistakes I think is down to a bit of human error... And I think the way that people can evaluate that is if they use the human element a bit more, and not just see humans as numbers, and create different products in the end."

The use of a richer understanding of the hidden drivers of human behaviour, actual outcome-based data, and a growth mindset approach to delivering marginal gains, are test-tube behaviours baked into the approach of the FANGs and subsequently other Silicon Valley start-ups. They give every employee the power to conduct tests, to build the evidence base for their theories and create products that pass this human test.

And this is something every business can learn from.

Having successfully built habit-forming, addictive products worth billions of dollars, the FANGs have not had solely positive impacts on society. Before embarking on influencing behaviour in digital and elsewhere, there are important ethical and moral questions to consider, which we will explore next.

CHAPTER 7

The Dark (and Light) Side of Digital – a Warning About Ethically Influencing Behaviour

THE INHERENT PROPERTIES of digital channels – the ability to collate data on actual behaviour, and to tailor experiences and messages accordingly – make adopting test-tube behaviours not only easier, but a practical necessity to achieve business success. But this does not just apply to the digital world – testing, learning and optimising based on behavioural data can be applied to deliver better experiences in a wide range of business contexts.

However, there are a range of associated ethical questions. Leaving aside the morality of influencing the decision-making of others per se, the collection of data for use in nudging behaviour – as well as creating addictive products and services – is rife for exploitation.

Betting companies use data to encourage bettors to spend more at online casinos. The Chinese government is collating data to inform its social credit system, rewarding citizens for 'good' behaviour – and punishing the 'bad' through restricting access to certain services. And Facebook found itself at the centre of a PR storm in 2018, when user data was used to influence the outcome of elections.

Responsible businesses, therefore, need to ensure they are considering the implications of influencing behaviour in digital, otherwise they risk reputational damage – or worse. There are three key questions to consider, which we will explore in turn.

Are you using data ethically – and legally?

By empowering every individual in the company to conduct tests, Facebook has opened itself up to well-documented problems. From a user point of view, it means the versions of Facebook that you see, and I see, and our friends see, could all be different – depending on whether we are being experimented on or not. And the data that is collated is analysed and used to change how Facebook works, for everybody. By doing this, Facebook can isolate the effect of individual contextual factors and ensure that the version served to each user is the most addictive experience possible, and therefore the most profitable – because it is more valuable to advertisers.

Just because they can do this, does not mean they should. Mark Zuckerberg confirmed in the same Freakonomics interview that Facebook's business priority seemed to be removing red tape and approvals, not ethical concerns.

"If what you're doing is sensitive to people's information at all, then of course there are a bunch of checkpoints that you need to do before doing that," says Zuckerberg. "But people try out different ideas for how to suggest you better friends, or suggest you better communities, and that doesn't need to go through a lot of process at the company; people can just try those out, and we're trying out hundreds of different versions of things like that. And the idea is that cuts through red tape at the company. So now a given engineer, instead of having to get their manager and then their manager's manager and then me on board with changing the app, *they can just do it.*"

As a result of this policy, engineers started working with third party data companies, and integrating apps that allowed data collection from users and their friends. One of these was Cambridge Analytica. Having harvested data from individuals via Facebook (allegedly without their true consent), Cambridge Analytica were able to use this data to target them with messages that preyed on their deepest fears and anxieties. It is alleged that the behaviour they were nudging in some cases was anti-democratic – specifically encouraging people not to vote.

The 2018 scandal resulted in Zuckerberg having to give testimony before Congress for the breach of private data, and make a public apology where he backtracked on this delegation of responsibility for user testing: "It was my mistake, and I'm sorry. I started Facebook, I run it, and I'm responsible for what happens here."

Businesses who wish to behave ethically in digital – as they should – are understandably wary about the implications of this affair. That Facebook allowed this to happen, and with a House of Commons committee concluding that Mark Zuckerberg failed to show "leadership or personal responsibility" over fake news and the obtaining of personal data, has undermined faith in the platform – and wiped $100bn off the company value.

Most businesses are not engaged in anything as morally troubling or unethical as the activities of Cambridge Analytica. In fact, the original research pioneered by the Cambridge Psychometric Centre (CPC) at Cambridge University (which Cambridge Analytica then copied) has huge potential benefits for businesses.

The work shows that targeting individuals based on personality factors, using an established Big Five model,[68] can make advertising messages (for example) significantly more effective. In a test campaign for Hilton Hotels, via Facebook, the CPC showed that personality-matched ads delivered twice as many clicks and were shared three times as often as a control ad.

When the Cambridge Analytica scandal was in full swing in 2018, an editor from the news website Buzzfeed was interviewed on the BBC programme, *Newsnight*. He was sceptical that Cambridge Analytica had achieved the effects they claimed. "If this stuff works, why isn't Amazon doing it?" he said.

Well, as implied in the previous chapter, Amazon is notoriously secretive about how it uses data – so for all we know it is doing similar analysis. Plus, it has masses of data on what people are *actually buying*, so it doesn't need proxy data on personality or anything else.

---

68 The Big Five, or OCEAN, model is a validated psychological survey methodology that categorises personality factors into five broad categories: openness to experience, conscientiousness, extraversion, agreeableness and neuroticism. Research has shown these to be accurately profiled from a relatively small number of survey items (questions), and can give a wide range of insights into various behaviours and motivations. Openness to experience strongly indicates levels of political and social conservatism, for example, which seems to have been critical to Cambridge Analytica's analysis.

In the absence of data on actual behaviour, any media or advertising agency (for example) that seeks to deliver the best possible results for its clients should be using all available data and insights. Agencies will already be collating data from a wide variety of other sources to optimise in this way, and personality data is simply another weapon in the arsenal.

As Jeremy O'Grady said in his editorial in *The Week*: "Cambridge Analytica's crime is to have upended the myth of the rational voter and the rationalist rhetoric of newspapers and politicians; to have revealed a far more refined method of political seduction."

As a direct result of the Cambridge Analytica scandal, Facebook applied the new EU General Data Protection Regulation (GDPR) in all areas of operation, not just the EU. For businesses, the conclusion from this scandal is this: there are countless opportunities to use data to more effectively influence behaviour. But data should only be obtained with users informed consent, so that they can decide if they are comfortable with what sacrificing their data means.

Assuming this criterion is met, then the important, ethical questions businesses must ask themselves should be about the ends – not the means – to which data is put.

Are the outcomes of the behaviour positive or negative?

For My QuitBuddy, users readily gave us personal information on how much they spent on cigarettes, how much they smoked a day and so on, when they downloaded the app. They were not compelled to do so, and all data was anonymous, but users recognised the value exchange. By providing this information, the app provided a better, more tailored, experience, and made users more likely to achieve their objective in downloading the app: to quit successfully. If we had collected personality data to deliver that experience better, most users would likely have agreed to that also.

Nir Eyal, the author of *Hooked*, says that when building habit-forming products, makers need to ask themselves two questions to evaluate whether they are straying from influence into manipulation. First, "Would I use the product myself?" And second, "Will the product help users materially improve their lives?"

In the case of My QuitBuddy, the answer was a clear yes to both.

In the same way, businesses must be clear about why and how they are collating data, and ensure that it is to help an individual achieve their aims: be that a better experience or enabling them to purchase a desired product or service.

Where it becomes murkier is when using behavioural science and data strays into manipulation. Creating addictive products, be they digital products or cigarettes, implies that an element of agency has been lost. While behavioural science undermines the model of humans as rational individuals with total free will, when choice is deliberately removed, and makes our lives worse as a result, ethical red flags should rightly be raised.

Jason Smith leads a data innovation team at the data and credit scoring agency, Experian, having previously run a social media monitoring agency and worked with numerous other start-up businesses. He also produced a BBC radio documentary in 2018 on the light and dark side of social media, including the Cambridge Analytica scandal.

"It's quite scary to think how these models can manipulate people's behaviour," he says. "With Cambridge Analytica the scandal was really about misuse of data. We're not there yet, but when you have self-learning models that can automate that process, that automation puts it in a different category. We need to look at our value structures, so that when we use the technology we are using the tools to do things we want to do."

One scary example is a 2016 Google thought experiment, euphemistically called 'Project X', that openly hypothesised behavioural data being "given a volition or purpose rather than simply acting as a historical reference," that "reflect Google's values as an organisation." In effect, if Google decided as a company it wanted to address a societal problem like global warming, or, alternatively, endorse a political candidate that would give them a massive tax break, this suggested it could use data and automated processes to achieve that end. Given the wealth of data at their disposal, this potential manipulation is troubling.[69]

In terms of building addictive products, Facebook beats the other FANG companies hands down. It is also the product whose societal and behavioural outcomes are not obviously positive. Released in January 2019, a University College London social media study with 11,000 respondents found that 14-year-olds who spent more than five hours a day on social

---

69 If you want to know the totality of all the data Google has on you, you can download it at: takeout.google.com/settings/takeout. Tip: pour yourself a stiff drink first.

media were twice as likely to be depressed as those that didn't, with girls particularly badly affected. Time spent on social media was also linked to an increased likelihood of being the victim of online harassment or bullying, which also had associations with depression and poor sleep patterns.[70]

In 2013, when I was in Australia, we received a brief to try and use the pervasive, addictive nature of social media to achieve positive ends, and combat some of these negative behaviours. The Australian Government had, for several years, been running a campaign to try and address disrespectful relationship behaviour amongst teenagers, such as cyber-bullying and sharing pictures (e.g. nude selfies) without permission.[71] Called 'The Line', this sought to encourage teenagers to consider whether their behaviour was appropriate (i.e. whether they were crossing the line). Since the vast majority of teenage interactions are now happening in the digital, not physical, world, this was where our campaign focused.

The campaign faced several challenges. One is that telling teenagers what to do, particularly by an authority figure such as the government, can often have the reverse effect to that intended – known as reactance, a kind of reverse authority bias (see below). Another was that simply telling people what to do had a limited effect – as we have seen behavioural science shows that how you say something is as important as what you are saying. Besides these, in the social media sphere, there is far less control over the message – while the campaign was heavily monitored, teens were free to comment, subvert, or talk about the campaign as they wished.

On our side was the fact that, like most anti-social behaviour, it was actually a minority of teens who were being disrespectful to others. Most knew exactly where the line was, and could correctly define it, so we wanted to leverage those social norms. Knowing that we needed to, as far as possible, dissociate the government from the campaign, our strategy was to enable kids to define the line themselves – and provide the right prompts and tools to do so.

At the time, teen conversations were littered with acronyms like 'LOL', 'WTF', and the like. We created our own ('XTL' aka 'crossed the line') as a mechanism to allow teens to have a handy shorthand to call

---

70 www.thelancet.com/journals/eclinm/article/PIIS2589-5370(18)30060-9/fulltext
71 The insight behind this is that more serious adult behaviours – such as domestic and sexual violence – are heavily influenced by people's first experiences of romantic relationships, typically in their teenage years. By encouraging better behaviours at that age, it can lead to better outcomes later in life.

out unacceptable behaviour online.[72] We then seeded that in the social media world, to make it seem like it had arrived organically. Influential vloggers and bloggers among teens, like Troye Sivan, composed pieces on their experiences of inappropriate relationship behaviour, and celebrities like Ed Sheeran answered questions online about what behaviour was "XTL or not"?[73]

Whilst it is nigh on impossible to say whether it actually reduced disrespectful behaviour among teens, the term caught on. Again, the beauty of this was we could collect actual data on behaviour – use of the term XTL – as well as see how it was being used, and in what context. It also alerted us to potential disrespectful or abusive behaviour, which could be reported if necessary.

The term was used 21m times in social media, with 90% of teens using it in the right context. The campaign won Global Media Campaign of the Year in 2014 but, most importantly, it was clear that teens were actually using it to self-police, define when the line had been crossed, and call out unacceptable behaviour. Although the term may not have stuck around much beyond that year, it shows that – like all technology – social media has the power to do good, as well as evil.

Businesses should accordingly ask the question whether the behaviours they are seeking to drive with their products and services – in digital or otherwise – are beneficial for the business and customers. Unless it is a win-win for both, then the ends may not be justifying the means.

If the product is addictive, and the use of data is automated through machine learning tools, any negative consequences will simply be magnified.

AUTHORITY BIAS

As you are reading, imagine this scenario. A casually-dressed stranger runs in to the room (or on to the bus/train) and shouts urgently: "Get out, now!"

---

72 If we were creating the campaign again now, in 2019, the most effective vehicle for this would probably be an emoji.

73 This probably sounds slightly more impressive than it was, because at the time Ed Sheeran was not the massive megastar that he is at time of writing. Still, credit for him for doing this for the campaign, and, on a personal level, for being a fellow son of Suffolk and Ipswich Town fan (not the easiest lately).

What do you do? Do you obey? Do you ask why? Your first thought may be to wonder how the hell they got into your house. Either way, you will likely hesitate before obeying – if you do at all.

Now imagine the same scenario, but the person is now a police officer in full uniform. What do you do?

Likely you would do what they say. This is an example of authority bias: our tendency to be more strongly influenced by those with perceived authority. Like many behavioural biases, this is generally a good heuristic to have – in an emergency, it is sensible to do what a greater perceived authority suggests (because of their position, knowledge or experience). We should generally take the advice of our doctor if we want to lead a healthy life.

This tendency to compliance often operates subconsciously. An experiment found that people were three and a half times more likely to follow a man across the road into traffic if he was wearing business attire (suit and tie) than if he were dressed casually.[74] Shops now frequently use cardboard cut-outs of police officers to deter shoplifters.[75]

Every day, we make countless decisions – taking the advice of others is often necessary (and advisable) to help us avoid the paradox of choice (see page 50). As we will see in part six, brands often operate as heuristics, and seek to maximise authority by association, relevant to the context. For instance, toothpaste brands include dentists in white coats in advertisements to communicate how to prevent tooth decay – if they want to communicate how great it makes your teeth feel, then the best authority is an ordinary member of the public.

It is not just uniforms that have this effect. Top NBA basketball stars LeBron James and Dwayne Wade wear glasses off the court – despite having 20/20 vision. They admitted this is because they are aware of the heuristic that people with glasses are perceived as more academic and intelligent. They wear spectacle frames

---

74 Lefkowitz, M., Blake, R. R., & Mouton, J. S. (1955). Status factors in pedestrian violation of traffic signals. *The Journal of Abnormal and Social Psychology*, 51(3), 704-706.

75 My friend and colleague Steve Thompson tells a story about an acquaintance who was getting frustrated by the number of items being 'borrowed' from the AirBnB apartment they owned. They put a selfie of them with a policeman in a frame on a prominent shelf in the apartment, and the thefts stopped immediately.

(with no lenses) to remind others that they are articulate college graduates, attract more sponsors, and (more altruistically) to send a subconscious message to poor black youth in the US that academia is as valid a route to success as professional sport.[76]

This deep-seated deference to any perceived authority is not always a good thing. Stanley Milgram found in his ground-breaking 1961 experiments that people could be so influenced by a man in a white coat that they would deliver fatal electric shocks to someone they did not know and could not see.[77] He wanted to demonstrate how seemingly normal (i.e. non-sociopathic) people could be compelled to commit horrendously immoral acts – with particular reference to the Holocaust.

Accordingly, mindless deference can impede effective decision-making in business. The HiPPO effect describes when stakeholders are most influenced by the highest-paid person's opinion (HiPPO). But those people may have totally fabricated or exaggerated their qualifications or competencies – 10% of CVs contain fiction of this type.[78] At the very least, other people in the organisation may have more expertise on a specific issue.

Every day we can read stories about examples of CEO corruption or incompetence, and know that blind obedience to authority is not always the wisest course of action.

---

76 You may have noted from my author photo that I am a glasses wearer. Although aware of this heuristic, I do actually need these to see, and for complex medical reasons cannot use contact lenses. Burdened with the (minor) disability of short-sightedness since childhood, I find the phenomenon of hipsters wearing glasses for purely aesthetic reasons somewhat offensive, but I think I'm in the minority on this issue (I give James and Wade a pass for the reasons cited above).

77 The methodology used in the most famous Milgram experiment involved an 'experimenter' in a white coat instructing participants (teachers) to administer increasingly high electric shocks to a test subject (learner) in an adjacent room, as a result of him giving incorrect answers to a test. If they protested, they were given verbal prods to continue and reassured by the experimenter. In reality, the learner was an actor and no shocks were administered, but teachers heard his (fake) reactions and protests. Despite this, the first set of experiments found 65% of teachers administered the maximum 450-volt shock. The experiment is controversial, both on ethical grounds (preventing it being fully replicated more recently) and due to questions over validity, but it remains one of the most cited, and (in)famous, social psychology experiments.

78 yougov.co.uk/topics/politics/articles-reports/2017/06/20/what-are-most-common-lies-people-tell-their-cvs Important to note that 10% of people admit to lying on their CV. The proportion of people who actually lie is potentially higher.

What are the implications of creating an addictive product or service?

If you listen to Mark Zuckerberg, he simply created an innovative piece of tech that enabled the world to "connect".[79] Well, that wasn't particularly novel in 2005. We had Myspace, Friends Reunited and Bebo for that. Hell, you could message your friends in real time on Instant Messenger, long before Facebook Messenger launched in 2011.

But what Facebook did better than those other businesses was create a far more addictive product – one which leveraged behavioural science principles to create something people could not live without. What has come to light recently is that, once they realised it had this effect, that became their business strategy.

At an Axios event in 2017, Facebook co-founder Sean Parker[80] said: "You're exploiting a vulnerability in human psychology. The inventors understood this – and we did it anyway."

Why? To get users spending as much time on the app as possible: "The thought process that went into building these applications, Facebook being the first of them … was all about: 'How do we consume as much of your time and conscious attention as possible?'"[81]

In a BBC *Panorama* documentary in July 2018 about smartphone addiction, Hilary Andersson spoke to a number of former executives about their time at the company, and their concerns about creating such an addictive product. Sandy Parakilas, a former product manager at Facebook, explained it thus: "Their goal is to addict you and then sell your time." Aza Raskin, the inventor of the endless scroll functionality,[82] became so concerned about the power of Facebook to generate addictive behaviour, he created the Center for Humane Technology: "We didn't realise that it

---

79   Their official corporate slogan/mission is "Facebook is a social utility that connects you with the people around you."
80   Possibly better known as the billionaire founder of Napster – and as the role played by Justin Timberlake in the movie *The Social Network*.
81   www.axios.com/sean-parker-unloads-on-facebook-god-only-knows-what-its-doing-to-our-childrens-brains-1513306792-f855e7b4-4e99-4d60-8d51-2775559c2671.html
82   This is the feature (now copied by other social networks) whereby more content endlessly loads when a user reaches the bottom of the screen. He uses the analogy of a soup bowl that never empties (because it is being secretly filled from below) – some behavioural experiments have demonstrated that in this scenario people eat far more than normal as there is no feedback mechanism telling them they have finished.

became so powerful that it addicts people," he says. "[Facebook is the] largest behavioural experiment we've ever seen. It's as if they're taking behavioural cocaine and sprinkling it all over your interface."

Everything on Facebook, from the prompt in the status bar of 'What's on your mind, Richard?' through to the content that populates my news feed, and in what order, has been carefully calibrated to generate an addictive experience – to keep me coming back for my next fix, make me click on a blue thumb, stop me going elsewhere, and make me a more valuable user to feed Facebook's business model.

Such is the importance of this that, in 2017, Facebook re-calibrated its algorithms so that users would start seeing more addictive content (i.e. from friends) in their news feed, and much less unwanted and unsolicited content from advertisers. Like Google persisting with the 'I'm Feeling Lucky' button, the short-term impact on advertising revenue was sacrificed for maintaining long-term usage and profitability.

A measure of the level of addiction of Facebook's more than 1bn active users was demonstrated in an experiment by *Nudge* co-author Cass Sunstein.[83] He asked Facebook users how much they would be willing to pay for the formerly free service. The average answer was $1 a month.

Not a lot, you might think, but probably reflective of how people recognise that Facebook is, at best, a mixed blessing in terms of impact on our overall health and wellbeing. This figure is given much greater meaning when compared with the average amount people were willing to accept to *stop* being able to use Facebook: $59 a month.

Like a true addict, we know that our habit is potentially causing us harm. But don't you dare try to take it away from us.

If you want to understand how valuable behavioural science is to a digital business – there's your answer. Creating a product people want might make you a few million dollars. But creating one that people can't live without – that could make you 59 times richer.

Combine this with the other behavioural insights we have seen in this part of the book, and the implications are clear. Creating digital products and services using behavioural data can drive positive behaviours, but, as Professor Shoshana Zuboff from Harvard Business School claims, we are in danger of it ushering in "an age of surveillance capitalism." In the next part,

---

83   papers.ssrn.com/sol3/papers.cfm?abstract_id=3173687. Sunstein explains this in terms of a super-endowment effect – reflecting people's resentment at having something taken away made them give protest answers.

we shall see that the rush for businesses to automate using the capabilities of machine learning and AI simply mean that this is now happening faster, at greater scale.

Accordingly, if your goal is simply to get rich, and you want to understand how a group of geeks from Silicon Valley became some of the richest people in the world – there's clearly far more to be learnt from a psychology textbook than there is from a computer science one.[84]

But, if you ignore the moral and ethical implications, you may still get rich – but you could end up in jail.

---

84   Zuckerberg, Page and Brin all dropped out of their college computer science courses, after all.

CHAPTER 8
Behavioural Science in Digital

WHAT TO DO NOW

I N THIS PART we have seen that behavioural science has driven the growth of the leading digital companies (the FANGs) in the 21st century by:

- providing an evidence-based understanding of the psychology of consumers to create products and experiences that are more useful, memorable, cognitively effortless and therefore more addictive than their competitors;

- using data to create personalised products and leverage social proof;

- cultivating a growth mindset within their organisation that encourages testing and experimentation based on actual user behavioural data, to enable evidence-based decision-making, i.e. test-tube behaviours.

Consequently, there are a number of ways to make effective use of behavioural science in digital to grow your business:

- focus on creating cognitively easy and effortless digital products and services;

- use actual data on behaviour to test hypotheses, to inform personalised products and services, and nudge usage;

- ensure test-tube behaviours become habits for everyone in your business.

However, we have also seen that this approach raises important ethical questions, and that businesses need to meet three key criteria to avoid possibly irreparable damage:

- Are you using data ethically and legally (i.e. collecting with clear consent and being transparent about how the data will be used)?
- Are the behavioural outcomes you are seeking positive? Ask: would you use the product or service, and will it materially improve users' lives?
- What are the implications of creating an addictive product? Will it have a net positive impact on society?

PART
THREE

How Behavioural
Science Helps Us Better
Understand AI, Robots
– and People

CHAPTER 9
Humans Versus Machines –
How Behavioural Science
Creates Better Products and
Services for Humans, and
Robots

Monkeys, cucumbers, and grapes

O NE OF THE most effective videos I use when training customer service staff is a YouTube clip from a TED talk by Dutch evolutionary biologist, Professor Frans De Waal.[85] De Waal and colleagues do extraordinary work with animals understanding the evolutionary basis for some of our most prevalent, system-1 biases.

In the video, two capuchin monkeys that live in the same social group are side-by-side in Perspex cages.[86] De Waal explains that monkeys really enjoy eating grapes, which are sweet, juicy and delicious, but will happily also eat cucumber – they just don't like it anywhere near as much. The

---

85   I first saw this in a presentation by Rory Sutherland in Sydney in 2014. The clip has been viewed over 14m times, probably not only because of its relevance to understanding human behaviour. Monkeys behaving badly is inherently hilarious – I'm not really sure why.
86   They do not live in these cages, they are only placed in them temporarily for this experiment, before returning to a large compound.

scientist feeds them cucumber through a hole in the cage, wearing a kind of face-protecting riot mask – for reasons that soon become clear.

The monkeys are rewarded with cucumber for completing a simple task – passing a small stone to the scientist. They happily eat this, as they have on the previous ten occasions. Then there's a switch: the monkey on the right gets fed a grape for the same task. The other monkey sees this, but when she next hands over the stone, she receives cucumber – not a grape, like her friend.

The response is hilarious and instant. The monkey puts its hand through the cage aperture and, in a fit of rage, throws the cucumber slice at the scientist (hence the mask). After seeing the monkey on the right receive a grape a second time, the other monkey first tests her stone against a wall as if to see if there is some kind of prank being played. And when she is again unjustly rewarded with cucumber, throws it again and rattles the cage in sheer righteous anger – like a hairy Hulk.[87]

I use this in training (other than for light relief), because it illustrates the point that behavioural biases – in this case, our innate sense of fairness and desire for equal treatment – are a product of our evolution. Capuchin monkeys are some of our nearest evolutionary ancestors, but De Waal says this experiment has also been replicated with cats, dogs and birds.[88] This explains both why biases are so prevalent and so strongly felt – they have been hard-wired into us for millennia. In training someone will often remark how similar the monkey's behaviour is to a customer ranting down the phone at them – when people feel they have got a raw deal, they feel this emotion strongly, and react accordingly.

And as humans and social animals, we instinctively understand and recognise this response due to the empathy we feel to others.

Irrational human behaviour or 'bugs'?

One thing you notice in a call centre (for example) is that skilled customer service representatives can instinctively tell within a few seconds (or less) how a call is going to go – they pick up subtle voice cues that tell them if

---

87 As I understand it, the monkey is calmed by being given plentiful grapes afterwards.
88 I often tell people to remember this experiment if they have more than one pet and favour one over the other. Eventually Rover might snap and bite if he sees you keep giving Fido better (or more) food.

the caller is seething with rage about a perceived injustice, and adapt their tone of voice and responses accordingly. To deliver a good service they will reflect this in their own tone and language (the psychological technique known as mirroring), and respond sympathetically.

In the project described in part one, when working with a call centre for one of the UK's largest savings banks, there was a large discrepancy between the typical age of callers and that of the staff. The oldest caller I heard was 97 years old, and some call centre staff were recent school leavers – an age gap of 80 years! Some calls were complex, requiring rigorous security processes, meaning a lot of calls were an exercise in patience for both parties.

To a certain extent, these problems were addressed successfully through the previously described script changes, which put customers at ease, recognised their more emotional, system-1 behaviours and better explained the processes. But it was clear that some more instinctive, 'softer' skills were also required. One of the best CSRs I listened to was a young student (studying part-time), who was endlessly patient, helpful and highly effective at dealing with the more difficult, older customers.

I asked how she was able to keep calm and still deliver great service after a lengthy, challenging conversation with a customer.

"I just imagined I was talking to my grandmother," she said.

This is a great example of the differences between human-to-human and human-to-robot interaction, and how businesses often underestimate the importance of psychological and behavioural factors in creating better experiences for customers (humans). In this case, the CSR was one of the best performers because she had empathy with customers, and the technique used – imagining she was talking to an elderly relative – was one others could learn from.

An automated, generic response from a digital robot assistant (a chatbot) – a cheery "How are you today?" for example – that shows no empathy with a customer complaint, will simply deepen their anger, not lessen it. The 'computer says no' response immortalised in the famous *Little Britain* sketch struck a chord precisely because it reflects the type of experience we have all had – where a product, service or system has been designed without an understanding of the humans using it. These lead to a significantly worse experience, and likely lose a business a customer (or several, if they tell their friends about it on social media).

To these systems (and the engineers who create them), a non-rational, emotional human response is often simply seen as a bug. Yet this is the very thing that makes us human, a product of thousands of years of evolution, and distinguishes us from the fictional, Spock-like, emotional vacuum of neoclassical economic thinking.

The AI gold rush

Despite these frequent 'computer says no' scenarios, businesses are still rushing to introduce automated processes. In 2018 and 2019, I attended the CogX conference in London, a huge 'Festival of AI and Emerging Technology' organised by CognitionX, where speakers and delegates from around the world convened to learn about potential applications. The 2019 event had 15,000 attendees and 500 speakers. A chatbot specific summit I attended in Berlin in June 2017 had 1,500 delegates, and over 50 different exhibitors.

In 'narrow' AI – using machine-learning technology for the application of simple rules and facts at speed and scale – there are obvious efficiency savings for business. The manufacturing industry has been transformed by the use of robots that can reproduce simple processes more quickly, accurately and reliably than humans. In retail, Amazon's processes are almost entirely automated – the only humans involved between you placing your order and receiving it are in the warehouse and driving the delivery vehicle – and Amazon are working on delivery drones and other technology to replace those roles in the near future.

In the customer service sector, Julian Harris (formerly head of technology AI research at CognitionX) shared with me an example of how a 12-person team in a call centre was now able to handle the same volume of calls, to the same level of customer satisfaction, as a 300-person team, through replacing human agents with chatbots. Once an avatar that could respond to emotional cues was introduced – showing a limited form of empathy – this increased overall customer satisfaction by 10%.

My experience is that in the customer service world there is an arms race to introduce chat-based technology, and replace phone-based contact centres. There are enormous cost savings to be made having thousands of daily customer queries dealt with by a computer in a cupboard, rather than by hundreds of low-wage workers in a call centre, and it partially reflects consumer trends of moving from offline to online transactions. But businesses are rushing to adopt the technology having been largely sold on the financial benefits, without considering the longer-term impacts on wellbeing, brand perception and profitability. As we have seen, building a digital solution without first considering the behavioural and human challenges will lead to a solution that prioritises efficiency over effectiveness.

An Ask Jeeves, rather than a Google.

Simply employing a robot to do a human's job with no consideration of the behavioural challenges involved will always be ineffective, both for your customers and employees. In customer service, a function that exists to meet the (frequently emotional) needs of human customers, these challenges are particularly acute.

Despite this, customer service is an industry that has been impacted by the use of automation faster and more deeply than most. Gartner, the analyst firm, estimate that by 2022, 72% of customer interactions will involve an emerging technology, such as a machine learning (ML) application, chatbot or mobile messaging – this is up from 11% in 2017. By 2021, 15% of customer service interactions are expected to be completely handled by AI, an increase of 400% from 2017. And phone-based communication will drop from 41% to 12% of overall customer service interactions.[89]

At the CogX conference, a substantial proportion of speakers and delegates were from the customer service world. As an industry, customer service is at the vanguard of automation, and is accordingly confronting the opportunities and challenges it brings head on.

Yet, the increasing use of automation via digital transformation programs has not led to widespread improvements in customer experience – the core purpose of customer service functions. The opposite is often true. We have all had experiences where, through an inability to find the right information, or comprehension of our query, we have had to revert to speaking to a human to get our query resolved to our satisfaction. The example Julian Harris gave above, where a limited form of empathy was integrated into the system, is the exception – not the rule.

The same Gartner research concluded that in 2021 a human agent will still be involved in 44% of all interactions – and that by 2020, 40% of bot/virtual assistant applications launched in 2018 will have been abandoned.

Rushing to automate without considering human behaviour, as in so many areas of business, is a quick route to bankruptcy. It is imperative to understand what distinguishes humans from machines, to build businesses that work for both.

---

89 'Gartner: Why humans will still be at the core of great CX', www.cmo.com.au, June 2018.

Humans versus algorithms

When the artificial intelligence in a driverless car is navigating the streets, it makes thousands of decisions every second based on predictions about how to safely reach its destination. Before changing lanes, it calculates the chances of an accident using a number of inputs (other cars, weather conditions and so on), combined with algorithms (rules) built from a database of outcomes of similar previous decisions.

Superficially, this may seem similar to how humans make decisions when driving. We assess the risks of our actions and predict the outcome based on experience. However, because we do not have similar data processing capacity – and fallible memories – we often make decisions using simple rules of thumb (heuristics and biases). And these can frequently lead us to behave in irrational, unpredictable and sub-optimal ways.

In 2016, I saw Daniel Kahneman interviewed at a conference in New York, where he was asked about the role of behavioural economics in a world where we are increasingly delegating decisions to algorithms. His response was a predictably pithy and brilliant one.

"The difference between an algorithm and a human," he said, "is that if you feed the same data into an algorithm twice you will get the same answer. This is not true of humans."

To put it another way, an algorithm (and the machine learning or artificial intelligence that relies on it) can only lead to rational, system-2 decisions, because of the rule-based, predictable nature of those decisions. An algorithm is simply a rule, and humans frequently break them. It struggles to cope when confronted with some of the irregularities and irrationalities of human behaviour – the very things that make us human.

Hence, some of the AI public relations disasters of the last few years. When Microsoft created its Tay AI chatbot, which anyone could interact with online (and thereby train it) – within 24 hours it had turned into a Nazi, started uttering horrendous racial slurs and had to be shut down. Uber's self-driving cars have been involved in several accidents, all of which were largely a result of irrational and unpredictable human behaviour (for example, a fatal accident in Phoenix was caused by a pedestrian walking out into the road in front of the car).

And when Amazon built an AI for processing CVs submitted in job applications, they quickly found that it was discriminating against women and had to shut it down. Its machine-learning algorithm determined that men were more likely to be successful based on historical data – due to the sexist biases inherent in existing recruitment practices – so prioritised applications from men accordingly. The existing biases were exaggerated, not removed, through using an algorithm.

Building an algorithm based on data from human decision-making will simply replicate the biases that those humans have, and magnify them, unless you design them out.

In tech parlance: garbage in, garbage out.

The limits of AI – a question of trust

These negative outcomes, and the ethical and societal implications, of replacing humans with machines (which we will explore in the next part), mean that changing a human-to-human interaction to a human-to-machine one has psychological implications that can limit its usefulness for business.

We might assume this is due to some innate preference on the part of a customer for speaking to humans, as opposed to robots (for example). We are social beings, after all, and maybe speaking to machines is just never as emotionally satisfying.

The evidence is actually that, in business, we are often perfectly happy dealing with robots *as long as they resolve our query satisfactorily*. Research from leading chat platform provider, LivePerson, found that one third of people in the UK wanted a chatbot to have a name and personality – but nearly half did not care in the least, as long as it resolved their issue (in the US the proportion was 57%). We are under few illusions as to the primary driver for businesses using a bot – 44% of Brits perceive that the only reason a company uses a bot is to save money.[90]

We are comfortable with a robot handling our queries for us, as our bigger concern is simply to receive service quickly and effectively (that companies make it easy). The challenge of integrating AI and automation into business is therefore a behavioural one, rather than purely economic.

---

90 LivePerson, 'How consumers view bots in customer care', 2017. By contrast, 55% think it is to deliver faster/better service. As we saw from the savings bank call centre example, speed often delivers an inherently better customer experience because we all have better things to do with our time. In that case, when we reduced the average handling time of calls, customer satisfaction levels went up, not down.

The root cause is that automated processes, informed as they are by the strict application of hard and fast rules in the form of algorithms, are innately logical and system-2 based. The often irrational, emotional or intuitive system-1 drivers, which are so influential on our behaviour, are simply errors to an algorithm-based robot.

And that (lack of) trust goes both ways. When the Uber self-driving car ran over that poor woman in Phoenix, the news coverage focused on how it would set back the cause of self-driving cars, how much further the technology has to go before it is ready for mass adoption, and how many more miles would need to be driven by the vehicles before we could consider them safe.

This type of coverage increases the mental availability[91] of self-driving cars causing fatal accidents amongst the general population, and decreases trust in them to drive us safely. A 2017 US survey by the AAA found that three quarters of drivers were afraid to ride in a self-driving car.[92]

In July 2018, Waymo, the former Google self-driving project that spun out to become a separate business under Alphabet, announced it has driven over 8m miles on public roads using its autonomous vehicles, and its vehicles were averaging 25,000 miles a day – without a single fatality. Overall, in the last five years, there have been only four recorded fatalities involving self-driving cars.

In 2016, there were 1.18 fatalities for every 100m miles that Americans drove – a total of over 37,000 people.[93]

Accordingly, we can confidently make the prediction that you are far less likely to die in a self-driving car than one you drove yourself. But until these technologies are 100% safe, there will always be an irrational, psychological barrier to adoption.

My friend Eaon Pritchard (whom we shall hear more from in part six) has a spin on a famous quote from data scientist, W. Edwards Deming, who said: "Without data you're just another person with an opinion."

Eaon changes this to: "Without a coherent model of human behaviour, you are just another AI with data."[94]

---

91   Explained on page 14.
92   newsroom.aaa.com/2017/03/americans-feel-unsafe-sharing-road-fully-self-driving-cars/
93   www.nhtsa.gov/press-releases/usdot-releases-2016-fatal-traffic-crash-data
94   Taken from Pritchard's excellent book: *Where Did It All Go Wrong? Adventures at the Dunning-Kruger Peak of Advertising.*

As Kahneman said, simply feeding the same data into an algorithm over and over again will repeatedly give you the same answer. Humans are not wired that way.

In the next chapter, we will explore how this difference not only defines when businesses can successfully employ automation and AI in business – but, in some contexts, also puts robots at a significant advantage.

CHAPTER 10
Predicting Behaviour and Eliminating Noise – Behavioural Science and Automation

Prediction machines

W E SAW IN the last part the example of Amazon Prime, where econometric modelling inaccurately forecast the long-term success of the product. A key benefit of behavioural science is it allows businesses to better predict how people will behave. This is because behaviour often runs counter to what we might logically expect, or what traditional economic models tell us, because humans are emotional, irrational and frequently counter-intuitive.

We are not rational, decision-making machines. Humans, like Homer, are from Earth and robots, like Spock, are from Vulcan.

The Australian academic Professor Joshua Gans[95] says that "prediction is valuable because it is an input into decision-making. It helps you make a better decision."

For businesses to make better decisions when designing processes, systems and communications, what they need is data. The better the data

---

95   Jeffrey Skoll, Chair in Technical Innovation and Entrepreneurship at the Rotman School of Management, University of Toronto and author of the book, *Prediction Machines*.

on past behaviour available (in both volume and relevancy), the more accurate those predictions will be.

Businesses like Netflix and Amazon use the tools of machine learning and artificial intelligence to process the billions of data points they possess, to build predictive algorithms (rules) to help them make better decisions, and to test their hypotheses – as well as to automate certain simple processes. Gans calls these 'prediction machines', because these algorithms make forecasts about the outcomes of decisions and optimise accordingly (based on definable trends in behavioural data). This is how Netflix has hundreds of millions of personalised products, rather than one.

But data is not enough on its own, as we have seen. Without the ability to process that data and generate new hypotheses for testing, a business cannot create the test-tube behaviours critical to success. Without an accurate understanding of human behaviour, informed by behavioural science, the hypotheses for testing will be rational, predictable, and the same as the competitors. Amazon Prime would never have been suggested without an understanding of 'the power of free', for example.

Any business that seeks to automate a process – be it a simple search algorithm on your website or creating a manufacturing robot – therefore needs to understand both the technological capabilities *and* human behaviour. Google's PageRank algorithm (for example) was successful because it was a cognitively easier way to present search results to users. Larry Page knew how people wanted information presented – because it was his PhD thesis – and designed the technology accordingly.

He built a prediction machine based on the behaviour, not the technology – and then used data to optimise it via experimentation.

Better predictions with behavioural science

I was presenting at a conference on some of the limitations of AI, and why we should understand humans better before designing technological business solutions, when I was asked: if we want to create services and processes that better adapt to the irrationalities of human behaviour, don't we just need better AI feeding off better data sets? In essence, we just need better prediction machines?

The world of customer experience shows we are still a long way off solving that problem – if we ever will. A call centre agent can accurately tell the nature of a call almost instantaneously, and react accordingly. Until technologists solve the Turing Test,[96] AI-driven, chatbot technology cannot.

Chatbot technology in customer service has thus far been limited to simple, generic customer requests (notification of a change of address, for example) using narrow AI, despite the incredible advances being made in AI and tech generally. In 2017, I spoke to a leading mobile phone company about behaviourally optimising their customer service chatbot. At the time, it was limited to handling 20% of all customer queries simply because they had to fit one of these neat categories. For these simple types of request, customers are generally comfortable with a robot handling it as our primary concern is simply to receive the service quickly and effectively (that companies make it easy).

I asked how they had developed the script to use in these cases. "We asked our best CSR to write down what she says," was the reply. "And used that." Needless to say, this completely ignores the differing nature of human-to-human and human-to-robot interactions.

It might seem a logical approach for a business to grow the use of this tech over time, as it gets more sophisticated and learns from more data. Julian Harris says: "The aggregate data you collect from your users, overall, has a substantial influence on the experience of an individual's use of your system." But for more complex requests, there are inherent biases that influence our behaviour differently depending on whether we are speaking to a human or a robot, and so it is simply not effective to replicate what a human would say.

"I can't use AI to sort out more complicated questions, because that would involve critical thinking or symbolic analysis. That is an area where you need to speak to a human. These are questions where there is no right or wrong answer," says Gartner VP Michael Maoz.

"If I'm also trying to build a relationship, and I don't have enough data, a human can reach out and build that relationship. I could let you do it

---

96 The Turing Test, developed by Alan Turing in 1950, is a test of a machine's ability to show intelligence that is equivalent to a human. The test is passed when a human cannot tell whether it is speaking to a machine or another human, and, although controversial, is still an important concept in the field of artificial intelligence, and as yet unsolved. Turing referred to this as 'the imitation game', which became the title of the 2014 movie biopic about his life starring Benedict Cumberbatch.

yourself, but for the relationship, I would prefer to bring in a human to grow the business."[97]

"The challenge to address is to avoid getting unrealistic expectations around emotion," says Harris. "One of the reasons why we had a number of AI winters across the world – where basically people lost interest and walked away from it – was that people thought it could do something more generally, when it turned out it only worked in a few specific examples."

When I asked Harris about this problem, he said that most businesses were trying to solve it by looking at either facial recognition (looking at expressions) or tone of voice technology, and correlating that to our emotional responses. The technology is not yet sophisticated enough to be accurate – in one case CognitionX found a product suggested with 95% accuracy that a call centre agent was angry during a perfectly calm, normal call. There is likewise no one facial expression or tone that universally represents anger – it is an amalgam of many factors – making it an extremely hard problem.

"The industry's there, and people can plug it in, and you can get a signal, I just wouldn't trust that signal until I can validate it with my particular case," he adds. "When there is a low commitment to the outcome I would be less concerned about the use of emotion detection, but I would be much more concerned about using the technology as a basis for parole decisions, for example."

There are a number of simple, transactional scenarios where technology has already created better products and services. Satellite navigation systems. Voice activated technology, like Alexa and Google Assistant, allowing you to search for information when your hands are full. A simple change of address request with your utility provider through a chatbot. Booking a ticket for the cinema on the phone.

These are not complex behaviours, and the technology required is at best very narrow AI – there is very little learning involved, nor insights into human behaviour. For harder behavioural problems – a customer complaint, planning a journey based on comfort rather than speed – what is needed is, to use tech parlance, better 'training data' (examples of relevant conversation). That is, data that reflects the emotional and irrational drivers of human behaviour.

---

97   Gartner (2018).

Until that training data is found, these problems are only solved by a human using empathy, creative thinking and emotional intelligence.

Removing 'noise'

If businesses can design better solutions based on insights into nonconscious drivers of behaviour, recognising the importance of context, then the opportunities for AI are much greater. Because ultimately, in most cases, humans just want their lives made easy – and behavioural science provides the most accurate training data on cognitive ease, as we have seen throughout this book.

Kahneman says that the inconsistency of responses to stimuli is the thing that separates humans from algorithms. As we will now see, for those simple, rule-based problems in business which require consistent and efficient processes, this can actually be a significant advantage of robots over humans.

As I say in my work in customer service: one good thing about a chatbot is they always stick to the script.

When I saw Daniel Kahneman in conversation with Nate Silver[98] at the same conference in 2016, he talked about 'noise'. By this, he meant things that affect our decision-making that we would not want to be affected by – heuristics that make us inaccurate in our predictions, and create what he calls 'useless variability'. These are what differentiate us from robots, and affect human ability as prediction machines.[99]

This is not uncontroversial – our heuristics and biases perform important roles, and without them we would be unable to function.[100] The world is

---

98   Nate Silver is a US statistician and polling expert, and creator of fivethirtyeight.com, a website devoted to statistical modelling and analysis of politics and sport. Famously, his statistical model correctly predicted the outcome in 49 of 50 states in the 2008 US Presidential Election, and all 50 (plus the District of Columbia) in 2012. In 2016, although this model predicted a Clinton win – as everyone else did – it gave an increasing (but still slight) chance every day beforehand of Trump winning the electoral college, but losing the popular vote (up to 25% by election day). Which was exactly what happened.

99   Richard Thaler has a similar analogy that he referenced in his Nobel Prize acceptance speech: 'Supposedly Irrelevant Factors' (SIFs). Behavioural biases are SIFs, in that they are things that the traditional, neoclassical economic view of the world considered to be irrelevant to how people behave.

100 Not that Kahneman or Thaler would dispute this point either, but some academics (most notably Gerd Gigerenzer) have criticised the presumption that heuristics and biases necessarily lead to errors. Kahneman himself acknowledges as much – in *Thinking Fast and*

impossibly complex, and so decision-making would be impossible without them. We shall see in parts five and six that they help us decide what products and services we buy, and so are fundamental to businesses better understanding how to influence purchase decisions.

A world full of Spocks, where everyone behaved totally rationally, would be extremely dull aside from anything else. Everything businesses do would be based purely on economic utility. Rory Sutherland points out the discipline of marketing would simply not exist in that world, as there would be no point in a function that seeks to create the desire to purchase goods and services based on irrational, intangible factors like perceived value and status.

When the monkey gets angry about not receiving grapes, or a human shouts down the phone because of bad service, this emotional response has a certain logic. If we did not react angrily to injustice, there is a possibility that we might be taken advantage of precisely because we did not react. As the old saying goes: "the squeaky wheel gets the grease." We learn from childhood that if we complain loudly enough it often brings rewards.

Leaving aside these evolutionary arguments, there are multiple examples where noise creates errors. More importantly, for a business it creates inconsistency, which can be eliminated by creating, and sticking to, rule-based algorithms.

The dangers of inconsistency

In a car factory automation creates greater efficiency, but it also improves quality – because robots should produce a car to the same standard every time. If a chatbot uses the same script for the same type of interaction without fail, then it delivers a consistent level of service to every customer, good or bad. This certainty can have tremendous value in behavioural terms (see overleaf), as well as in terms of profitability. Lean and agile approaches in business, based on optimising processes, are grounded in standardisation. If every person in an organisation has a different way of performing a task, it is impossible to find ways to improve because it is essentially random.

Slow, he describes how a chess grandmaster largely plays using system-1 processing, as he is an expert player, and only uses system-2 processes for hard problems (thereby minimising cognitive effort). His heuristics are a result of expertise and practice, and are unlikely to feature errors. Everyday chess players would rely much more on system 2.

You cannot improve a process if there is no process.

You may have experienced a scenario in business where you have asked for a piece of information (a quote for a piece of work, for example) from two or more people in the same, or similar roles, and had widely different responses. This is because the task allows them some element of judgment – and whenever judgment is involved, there is the potential for bias and noise.

Some examples: when software developers were asked on two separate days to estimate the completion time for a given task, the hours they projected differed by 71%, on average. When pathologists made two assessments of the severity of biopsy results, the correlation between their ratings was only 0.61 (out of a perfect 1.0), indicating that they made inconsistent diagnoses extremely frequently.

Worrying though this is, Kahneman and colleagues' own research confirmed that within two major financial service organisations, the average variation between valuation of cases was 48% and 60%. Each case was worth hundreds of thousands of dollars, so the impact of this inconsistency on profitability was huge.

They also found that expertise had no bearing – time on the job did not reduce variation in decision-making.

This was a complete surprise to these organisations. Kahneman and colleagues put this down to over-confidence, and a consensus effect: "Experienced professionals tend to have high confidence in the accuracy of their own judgments, and they also have high regard for their colleagues' intelligence. This combination inevitably leads to an overestimation of agreement ... In most jobs people learn to make judgments by hearing managers and colleagues explain and criticize – a much less reliable source of knowledge than learning from one's mistakes," says Kahneman et al. "Long experience on a job always increases people's confidence in their judgments, but in the absence of rapid feedback, confidence is no guarantee of either accuracy or consensus."[101]

Noise exists because even experienced professionals do not learn from previous mistakes – critical to a growth mindset and a test-tube behaviour.

101　These quotes and examples are taken from an article in the *Harvard Business Review*, October 2016 edition: 'Noise: How to Overcome the High, Hidden Cost of Inconsistent Decision Making' by Daniel Kahneman, Andrew M. Rosenfield, Linnea Gandhi and Tom Blaser.

It is the Israeli fighter pilot training problem all over again: businesses frequently make decisions based on judgments, not evidence, which creates biased errors and inconsistency.

But technology, which tests, learns and optimises based on reasoned rules (algorithms), does not – and this is where it can deliver significant benefits to business.

CERTAINTY AND UNCERTAINTY

Certainty is an important concept in behavioural science. Heuristics and biases are aids to decision-making, but they only come into play when humans are making judgments in conditions of uncertainty. If we are sure of the best course of action, we have no need to engage any cognitive effort to help us make a decision. If we make a bet with a 100% chance of success, then it is quite literally a no-brainer.

We have a strong bias to avoid uncertainty where possible. If something moves from a certainty to an uncertainty, then it triggers our tendency towards loss aversion (see page 29) as we become more conscious of the risks involved.

Tversky and Kahneman use this example. Which of the following options do you prefer?

A. a guaranteed £30

B. an 80% chance to win £45, and a 20% chance to win nothing

They found 78% of participants chose option A, while only 22% chose option B. But the expected value (average win) of option B (£45 × 0.8 = £36) exceeds that of A by 20% – so the rational choice is option B.

For businesses, there are many implications of this innate preference for certainty. One of the characteristics of the taxi-hailing app, Uber, is that it provides certainty by showing users how far away their taxi is using a map and location tracking. Rory Sutherland points out that it has been possible to order a taxi by phone since the 1920s, but it is this additional certainty over the arrival time that users value more than the novelty of using an app – as opposed to the uncertainty caused by simply booking over the phone and anxiously awaiting the taxi's arrival.

Example of Uber taxi location tracking

Source: Uber

In parts five and six, we shall see that it is this desire for certainty that many customers seek. It drives our preference for existing, established brands. If we are making a good enough, choice-satisficing purchase decision then it makes sense to choose based on brands we have previously purchased that did the job well. For businesses, this is why providing consistently good products and services is so important.

If you have used your local cafe regularly for five years, and the coffee, food and service is always good, then you have no psychological incentive to try the new coffee shop on the corner. Because why take the risk on an unknown quantity?

Technology, behaviour and data

The most radical solution to inconsistency and over-confidence, as in the car factory, is to take humans out of the process altogether. As Kahneman observed, an algorithm gives you the same answer every time.

As we have seen, for a business this will be limited by what is both technologically possible, and how hard the problem is in behavioural terms. A decision that relies on lots of subjective judgments, multiple inputs, or requires softer skills like empathy and creativity, cannot easily be replaced by an algorithm. Simply replacing people with software also creates a host of other business and societal challenges, as we shall see in the next part.

But where a process is sufficiently consistent, based on reliable data, and objective, removing noise can be relatively simple. When you use a price comparison website to get a quote for home insurance, for example, by answering a few simple questions the algorithms will generate a number of quotes from different providers. Answer the questions a second time in the same manner and the quotes will likely stay the same. Go back and change your answers slightly, and the quotes may change (and you may game the system a little).

As narrow AI, there is no great intelligence sitting behind this system.[102] There are a set of rules (algorithms), and this prediction machine is making a simple calculation about the likelihood of you making a claim, i.e. your risk level. In many cases, this may not be based on actual data, but simply a few reasoned rules – heuristics such as living nearer the sea increases the chances of flooding – rather than statistical models based on data from previous cases. Kahneman and colleagues say that these kinds of models are about as accurate as taking a collection of rules and weighting them equally, without even looking at outcome data.[103]

This is much the same as how an insurance underwriter would have assessed your case 20 years ago. The difference is, these rules would have been in their head and therefore subject to bias – if you had asked two underwriters from the same firm, they would likely have given you two different quotes.

The insight is that your initial algorithms can be very simple as long as you can learn from them: "The bottom line here is that if you plan to use

---

102 Although there may be at an aggregate level, i.e. more sophisticated machine learning may be being used to optimise the quotes being provided across the entire site, to ensure you are more likely to choose a quote and not go elsewhere. Insurers may also be optimising quotes across all the different sites to maintain their overall risk at profitable levels. Which are much harder problems, involving millions of data points.

103 Kahneman et al., *Noise*. One of the examples used there is creating single aggregate numbers to predict the likely outcome of sports games – which is an approach pioneered by Nate Silver on his FiveThirtyEight site. It also reflects how credit ratings work, and the approach taken by the Oakland A's to assess baseball players as described in Michael Lewis's *Moneyball*, referenced later in part four.

an algorithm to reduce noise, you need not wait for outcome data. You can reap most of the benefits by using common sense to select variables and the simplest possible rule to combine them."[104]

As long as the data you use is unbiased, and the rules are simple, businesses can build prediction machines that get better over time, and are more consistent than a human.

Kate Glazebrook is the CEO and co-founder of Applied, a digital platform originally created at the BIT. Applied uses behavioural and data science to improve the quality of recruitment decisions, both making them less biased and improving the predictability of those decisions – thereby helping businesses avoid the problems Amazon faced with its sexist, AI application screening tool.

"We all tend to trust our judgment, probably a little bit more than we ought to," says Glazebrook. "And one of the things that we've thought quite hard about at Applied is … the point of studying behavioural science is not to create an 'us and them'. There is no such thing as a person that doesn't contain bias. There is no such thing as a process that doesn't. In fact, any process that's created by humans will inadvertently pick up the kinds of things that we've done in the past."[105]

But because of the heuristics that determine how we react to technology – the lack of trust that we saw in the previous chapter – the final decision will still need to be reviewed by a real, living human. As a car factory floor still has humans to maintain the machines, a business needs a human to run the rule over the prediction machines, and make sure the right (unbiased) training data is being applied. It also needs a human to provide accountability, as we will see in the next chapter.

Before rushing to build technological solutions, businesses therefore need to understand the limits of that technology, the behavioural biases inherent in using it and the biases within the data informing that technology. Should test-tube behaviours become habitual amongst a business's human staff – requiring, as it does, a richer understanding of the drivers of human behaviour and the use of data to test hypotheses – then these problems are avoided, as technology will never be developed for its own sake.

---

104 Kahneman et al., *Noise.*
105 In the next part, we shall see some of the specific biases that impact on recruitment decisions.

A technological solution should only be employed by a behavioural business if it works for the earthbound, Homer-like humans – as well as the space-dwelling, Spock-like robots.

And that means technology employed by business also has to meet human emotional and ethical standards, as we will explore in the next chapter.

CHAPTER 11

Artificial Irrationality – How Behavioural Science Helps Businesses Ethically Use AI and Automation

The importance of distinguishing between human and robot

L IKE AN ANGRY monkey with a piece of cucumber, humans have a strong emotional response to deception. As technology is increasingly blurring the line between human and robot interaction, and creating ever more lifelike robots and machines, we are more likely than ever to be unsure whether we are actually interacting with a human or not.

In May 2018 Google demoed their Duplex product, an artificial intelligence assistant that can call people up and interact with them, without knowing they were speaking to a robot. Chris Messina, the product designer most famous for inventing the social media hashtag, described the Duplex technology as "the most incredible, terrifying thing".[106]

Many commentators raised concerns about the ethics of people not knowing when they are speaking to a human or a robot, and that it

---

106 www.independent.co.uk/life-style/gadgets-and-tech/news/google-duplex-ai-artificial-intelligence-phone-call-robot-assistant-latest-update-a8342546.html. Google Duplex has since conceded that 25% of the calls are actually handled by people: www.google.com/amp/s/www.nytimes.com/2019/05/22/technology/personaltech/ai-google-duplex.amp.html

appeared to be deception by design. The website TechCrunch called it an "AI pantomime" and "worryingly suggestive of a company that views ethics as an after-the-fact consideration."[107] Google appeared to have been rushing to create the technology without any kind of ethical and value framework being applied.

As Jeff Goldblum memorably put it in the movie, *Jurassic Park*: "Your scientists were so preoccupied with whether or not they could, they didn't stop to think if they should."

As we get more used to these technologies over time, this instinctive response – the feeling of inherent *creepiness* – may lessen, in the same way that humans are slowly adopting voice-activated technologies like Amazon Alexa and Google Assistant. But with these, there is no doubt that it is technology we are engaging with, and we feel no deception.

There are parallels here with the uncanny valley; the concept that a robot cannot too closely resemble a human because it generates a sense of discomfort and unease. Uncertainty is a huge barrier to behaviour in many contexts and something we seek to avoid in decision-making.[108] It is also a barrier to adoption of technology.

Soul Machines, a New-Zealand-based company, is developing bio-mimicking avatars (including a baby simulator) which are so physically realistic as to be basically indistinguishable from humans. The baby simulator even includes a virtual nervous system.

Julian Harris (formerly head of technology AI research at CognitionX) said that despite this realism, it still generates a feeling of unease amongst people, simply because they know it's not real. "Unconsciously there's a whole pile of information that maybe the conscious mind doesn't even detect," he says. We are able to instinctively (i.e. on a system-1 basis) know when something isn't real, even if we can't articulate why.

In the same way, feeling uncertainty over whether we are speaking to a human or a bot will lead to uncertainty and therefore a worse experience – particularly if we are already feeling a sense of frustration, injustice or anger. If we feel deceived, the emotional, system-1 biases kick in.

Behavioural science ultimately tells us that humans want products and services that make life easy, and, to a certain extent, we do not care if these are provided through automation or not. The lesson for business is this: if

---

107   techcrunch.com/2018/05/10/duplex-shows-google-failing-at-ethical-and-creative-ai-design

108   See page 95.

you are deceptive about whether the customer is interacting with a human, you are not only delivering a worse experience, but potentially crossing an ethical line.

The ethics of AI and automation

Jason Smith said in the previous part of the book that automation of the collection and processing of data starts to put the activities of business into a different ethical category, particularly when it comes to use of self-learning models (i.e. beyond narrow AI). Businesses that are collating data unethically or illegally, generating negative behavioural outcomes, or creating addictive products and services, will simply be doing this faster by using AI-based technology – and, even more troublingly, without human oversight.

When I met with Smith, he was working on a new radio documentary about the ethics of AI and speaking to experts in the field. His findings were, to put it mildly, worrying.

"The important thing we need to address is the transparency within the self-learning models," he says. "We are going to have to explain how these models have come up with the decisions that they've made. We could have a backlash against models making decisions that no one quite gets … Inherently, the technology isn't bad. But are we going to apply it for a good use case? And can we create a framework that means that it is always guided towards being applied to the good use case?"

"We want to inspire people to focus on being sensible and ethical," says Julian Harris, who, prior to his role at CognitionX, spent seven years in global product roles at Google and implementing technology solutions for the UK government. "Working with AI technology has a new shape, driven by data. All data that humans touch is biased in some way. You need to make sure that for the purpose of your situation you have data that represents your intended outcome, and the nature of the people who are going to be benefiting from it. If you're a government, for example, it's important then that you really have a very comprehensive representation of data across the whole spectrum, as government has to include all people."

This highlights a major ethical – and business – challenge inherent in automation from a customer perspective. With 8% of the UK population never using the internet *at all*, there is a risk of leaving behind a whole group of customers by adopting technological solutions without considering the user base as a whole.[109]

Businesses must take the ethical AI lead

Kate Glazebrook explained to me the benefits of using diverse teams to build technological solutions that work for everyone.

"One of our clients has been trying to improve the rate at which women and minority groups apply to their tech roles," says Glazebrook. "Because as many of us know the technology industry is sadly one of the least diverse out there, which is important because technology increasingly shapes the way we all live. And so to have technology built by a very unique, narrow set of people runs the risk that we just don't build technology products that work for everyone. But one of the things that we have seen is, since using the [Applied] tool, this particular employer has seen a 25 to 30% increase in the number of women applying to technology jobs."

This is doubly important because having biased teams and data informing these models can result in terrible outcomes. The examples of the Tay chatbot and Amazon recruitment AI were bad enough, but a study published in March 2019 suggested that autonomous vehicles had more difficulty detecting people with dark skin than light skin. The research concluded that if you are black, you were 5% more likely to be run over by a self-driving car than if you were white.

In short, self-driving cars may be racist.[110] The only way to prevent these kinds of outcomes is to ensure the right value frameworks are in place to guide the collection and use of data before building the technology, not after. This consequence of biased data was not anticipated by the programmers and designers, and neither was the outcome. Only by putting the right incentives (either voluntarily or through regulation) in place beforehand can the 'garbage in, garbage out' problem be avoided.

---

109 Office for National Statistics, *Internet users*, UK: 2018. www.ons.gov.uk/businessindustryandtrade/itandinternetindustry/bulletins/internetusers/2018

110 www.businessinsider.com/self-driving-cars-worse-at-detecting-dark-skin-study-says-2019-3. The researchers suggested this was because the images used to train the systems had fewer dark-skinned pedestrians in them.

"There are very few regulatory bodies," says tech writer Paul Armstrong. "And I think that's why we've found ourselves in such disarray recently ... And if anything, it's almost giving [businesses] another free pass for another two or three years without repercussions ... It's always going to move in advance of the regulatory framework.

"We have to think of it more holistically. But that's quite hard to sell in when economic times are tough ... Could the change come from actual car regulators going: 'I won't be buying your software, because clearly it's racist.' So what is the pressure that you add to these companies? I think the answer we've seen in history is there's nothing that changes [behaviour] as quickly as taking money out of people's pockets."

How AI can help identify bias

There are three elements to building automated or AI tools: data, prediction and a decision. We have already seen that biased data can lead to terrible predictions and decisions. The additional problem is that, like self-driving cars, until we achieve 100% safety and accuracy, our biases mean we are more comfortable having decisions that affect us made by a fellow human. However much we remove biases from data and predictions, any decision needs to have a human involved, both to ensure that outcomes are optimised and to maintain accountability. And this requires understanding the (predictably irrational) drivers of human behaviour.

Julian Harris said in the previous chapter that the use of emotion recognition technology to determine someone's eligibility for parole would be concerning. This example was not plucked at random; research by Professor Sendhil Mullainathan[iii] and colleagues has shown that using machine learning algorithms to determine whether a judge should grant bail could reduce crime rates by 25% without increasing jailing rates, or reduce the amount of people jailed by 42% without increasing crime rates.[112]

As Mullainathan et al. conclude: "Good predictors do not necessarily improve decisions ... Predictive algorithms can serve as a behavioural diagnostic, helping to understand the nature of human error. Progress on these problems will require a synthesis of multiple perspectives, both

---

iii   Professor of Computation and Behavioral Science at the University of Chicago Booth School of Business.

112   cs.stanford.edu/~jure/pubs/bail-qje17.pdf

the techniques of machine learning as well as behavioural science and economics."[113]

In addition to removing noise, prediction machines can help us identify the biases in the first place. If a rational, rule-based algorithm does not impact behaviour in the way you might expect – bingo, there's your bias. This approach can help your business find more counter-intuitive solutions, just like Google did with the 'I'm Feeling Lucky' button.

"The information that you can derive from AI that's genuinely interesting – the most valuable information – is the counter-intuitive stuff that not everybody knows," says Rory Sutherland. "So if you could train AI to actually say: 'Okay, this is a chunk of all our prejudices, tell us what ain't so,' I'm actually quite interested in that."

Better training data – how behavioural science helps businesses ethically use AI and automation

In the case of granting parole, an algorithm may make fewer errors and be objectively better than a human, but the consequences of the errors are extremely serious. Releasing a murderer early could result in another murder. As with self-driving cars, if an error results in serious harm, it is front-page news. In those circumstances, who do we hold accountable? The creator of the algorithm? The data analyst?

In the case of the Uber crash in Phoenix, a US court concluded Uber were not legally responsible (though this may be overturned on appeal). The grape-loving monkey in all of us demands justice, and equal treatment in the eyes of the law, and businesses need to consider who will be accountable when algorithmic errors are made.

Much like a self-driving car needs a mechanism for drivers to take the controls if it is going to crash, a parole decision needs to be reviewed and approved by human experts. Both to provide accountability, and to make sure those human traits and irrationalities that system-2-based algorithms are blind to are taken account of, and ethical frameworks are adhered to.

---

113   Ibid.

For most businesses, the consequences of their decisions are not as serious, and so the opportunity is to use behavioural insights and machine learning to test, learn and optimise at an unprecedented speed and scale. For My QuitBuddy, described in part one, we optimised the app based on data and feedback from users. This was a largely manual process, involving looking at user data and predicting how we could improve the user experience of the app by tweaking its functions.

If we were launching the app again now, this process could be entirely automated. The app could be optimised in real time, with machine learning algorithms being used to update the functionality based on what users were interacting with, and updates served to the app stores automatically. Much as the Netflix user experience is tailored to each individual user.

This is the future for many businesses, where machine learning and AI can provide a way to embed test-tube behaviours, and test, learn and optimise faster and more accurately. Chatbots (for example) can adjust their responses based on what customers are responding most positively to, and tailor it to the individual customer's needs, using behavioural insights as well as data on that specific customer.

In summary, what behavioural science provides is the *most effective training data* to build models to inform machine learning and AI technology. And the better your training data, the better your prediction machine – and the greater the competitive advantage.

However, if that decision affects humans in any way, businesses need to ensure that there is human oversight to maintain accountability, and to provide the right empathetic and emotional responses.

Otherwise you might find your customers start throwing the cucumber around.

In the next part, we shall see that in addition to these limitations, replacing humans with robots without considering the behavioural implications can have major downsides for businesses and society – beyond just losing your job.

CHAPTER 12

AI, Automation and Behavioural Science

WHAT TO DO NOW

IN THIS PART, we have seen how behavioural science is critical to effectively employing automation and machine learning/artificial intelligence in business because:

- instinctive emotional responses and empathy are complex behavioural problems that can currently only be addressed by humans, rather than robots;

- automated customer service solutions (for example) will assume that customers are totally rational, system-2 (i.e. Spock-like) decision-makers, which is provably untrue;

- human-to-human interactions trigger certain behavioural biases that do not apply to human-to-robot interactions, and vice versa;

- it shows that we can eliminate noise (inconsistent decision-making) by applying algorithms in certain contexts;

- predictive algorithms cannot make decisions alone when they impact on outcomes for humans, because of our desire for accountability and intolerance for errors;

- these technologies allow businesses to test, learn and optimise based on actual behaviour (i.e. employ test-tube behaviours) at an unprecedented speed and scale;

- it allows us to ensure the predictions that algorithms make about human behaviour are more accurate, by creating more effective training data.

Consequently, there are a number of ways to make effective use of behavioural science alongside automation and AI to grow your business:

- ensure the right value frameworks are in place to guide the collection and use of data before you build your technology, not after;
- design better automated/AI solutions based on insights into subconscious drivers of human behaviour, to make cognitively easier products and services;
- recognise there are harder problems requiring empathy and emotional intelligence that only people can solve;
- if a process is sufficiently consistent, based on reliable data, and objective, then using algorithms can effectively remove noise;
- but these must also be subject to expert human review and a power of veto, to provide accountability.

However, again, this approach raises important ethical questions, and businesses need to think about whether they are not making explicit when humans are dealing with machines. Many humans consider this deceitful, find the uncertainty unsettling, and have strong negative emotional reactions to it.

PART
FOUR

Boosting Productivity
with Behavioural
Science

CHAPTER 13
The Rise of the Machines, and the Future of Work – Behavioural Science and a Changing Workforce

Will a robot be stealing your job?

B EHAVIOURAL SCIENCE CAN help businesses make best use of AI and automation (and humans) to create better products and services, but can it help with the other consequences of replacing human jobs? The Office for National Statistics (ONS) estimates that 1.5m people in England are at high risk of losing their jobs to automation (programs, algorithms or robots). This represents over 7% of the total workforce, with 70% of those roles currently being held by women.

"It is not so much that robots are taking over, but that routine and repetitive tasks can be carried out more quickly and efficiently by an algorithm written by a human, or a machine designed for one specific function," the ONS said. Jobs most at risk are those requiring less complexity, lower levels of formal education, and less experience, as the chart below shows. This is of greater concern for the next generation of workers – amongst 20–24-year-olds the proportion at risk of job automation is double the national average, at 16%.

Jobs at risk from automation

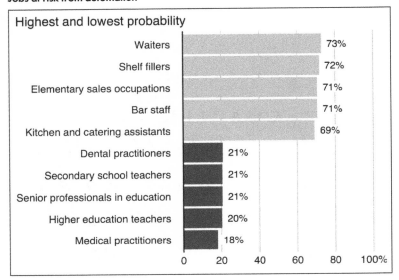

Source: Office for National Statistics [114]

You'll remember from a few pages ago that there are some aspects of work where machines are (currently) inferior to humans – roles requiring empathy and creativity, for example – but there are plenty of jobs performed by humans where these are not critical. In fact, many roles are better performed when human inconsistency and noise is removed altogether, as Daniel Kahneman has shown. Uber and others are investing millions of dollars in self-driving cars, because they can do the job more safely and efficiently than humans.

The impact of automation (both positive and negative) for business will depend on the nature of the business, and its objectives. For Uber, the objective is to provide a taxi service as cheaply as possible, and increase profitability by removing humans from the process.[115] As a society we may decide to encourage different, more effective and more sustainable behaviours to solve our transport problems, for example, such as encouraging people to use public transport.[116]

---

114   www.bbc.co.uk/news/business-47691078
115   In Uber's case, they first need to actually become profitable. In 2018, the business accrued a loss of over $1bn (source: Bloomberg).
116   A 2019 study concluded that in Uber and fellow ride-sharing app Lyft's home city of San

"The idea that the self-driving car has to be infrastructure independent strikes me as a sort of stupidly ambitious thing that seems to be driven by a mindset, and not really by a proper approach to problem solving," says Rory Sutherland.

Psychological solutions will be needed to solve economic problems

This is another example of how societal problems related to increasing automation, such as mass unemployment, could have more effective solutions grounded in psychology rather than economics.

The value of understanding the real (i.e. hidden) drivers of behaviour, and becoming a test-tube business, is it encourages you to look at problems differently. The examples in the last part show that the growth of automation in business is a double-edged sword – the efficiencies delivered by automation are not necessarily matched by corresponding improvements in effectiveness. Replacing a workforce with robots is not a like-for-like switch, as the incentives and motivations of humans are often irrational and/or emotionally driven, and the nature of human-to-robot interaction is very different to human-to-human.

A Royal Society of Arts, Manufacturers and Commerce (RSA) report from March 2019 predicted four possible futures of work in the UK in 2035. From this, forecasts on the proportion of jobs at risk from automation ranged hugely from 5–35%. The scenarios ranged from: a new machine age decreasing the costs of everyday items at the cost of mass unemployment; a future of "hyper surveillance"; an economic crash leading to a mass move to self-sufficiency and a return to an agrarian economy; and, optimistically, to "an empathy economy", with an increasing human focus on sectors like education, care and entertainment, with those roles becoming the majority of human jobs. Whilst the last is probably the most positive scenario, it "brings with it a new challenge of emotional labour" – that is the growth

---

Francisco they had increased, not lessened, the amount of congestion – contrary to claims by both companies. Between 2010 and 2016, traffic had increased in the city by 60%, with over half being directly as a result of Uber and Lyft. www.theverge.com/2019/5/8/18535627/uber-lyft-sf-traffic-congestion-increase-study

of human roles will be in "emotionally exhausting" (i.e. psychologically demanding) roles.[117]

"We know that artificial intelligence is a great tool to replace stuff that's process driven," says Jason Smith, who looked into these issues for his BBC radio documentary. "You could automate to actually do the jobs that we as humans don't really want to do. The stuff that humans are good at, the caring, the empathy, all those type of roles – we should start to place more value on those roles as a society and economy, because that's going to be our future. In some respects, artificial intelligence could allow us to find the very things that intrinsically make us human."

The conclusion is not just that many jobs will be lost to machines, but those that remain will have a greater psychological foundation, as they are roles that only humans can perform. It will only become more critical that businesses understand the drivers of behaviour, what motivates their customers and their staff, and how to keep them well and happy. Being in the behaviour business will not just be a 'nice to have' – but an essential.

But what about the people that are not able to be part of the empathy economy, the waiters and shelf fillers that are most at risk of automation? Can this be a positive development for them as well?

Losing your job to a robot may not be a bad thing – if it's a bad job

There are two problems businesses need to consider as a result of increasing automation. First, as we explored in the last part, the implications of replacing roles traditionally done by humans with machines, beyond simply delivering products and services more efficiently. Second, ensuring that those jobs that are left for humans, the things we are uniquely good at, constitute 'good' work. That is, work that keeps them healthy, happy and motivated, and therefore productive.

Behavioural science can help with both problems. A traditional, neoclassical economic response to the problem of mass unemployment from automation would be to focus on providing more of the jobs that can only be done by humans, and incentivising businesses to provide these.

---

117   www.thersa.org/globalassets/pdfs/reports/rsa_four-futures-of-work.pdf

This presumes that full employment, and the flawed metric of GDP, is the primary economic goal of a government.[118]

Such is the scale of the problem that even Bill Gates has suggested a robot tax to temporarily slow the spread of automation and fund other types of employment. Businesses who seek to replace humans with machines would have to pay a tax to do so, to finance care-giving roles such as looking after the elderly or children. This assumes that the role of business (the social contract) is to provide people with work, and that our only reason for working is financial gain – so, to attract people to empathy economy roles, we must simply pay them more. In the next chapter we shall see that money is actually a pretty ineffective motivator of behaviour in business. In any case, the rewards of this kind of work are largely emotional, not financial.

But what if we focus on those more emotional system-1 drivers of behaviour, and consider instead whether work makes people happy? Is work even *necessary* for people to not only survive, but to prosper?[119] If not, suddenly mass unemployment ceases to be a problem – especially if the jobs being replaced are dangerous, unpleasant or repetitive. Looking at the problem in this way, one solution proposed to the increasing loss of low-skilled jobs to automation is the introduction of a universal basic income (UBI) to replace the traditional scheme of benefits provided by government.[120]

The logic is this: every citizen, irrespective of needs or means, is given a subsistence level of income by the state (set just below the minimum wage), without condition. This ensures a basic level of living for all, whilst incentivising those who wish to work to do so. Having frequently been dismissed as one of the more wacky economic theories, in 2019 US Democratic presidential candidate Andrew Yang made this a unique cornerstone of his policy, and Shadow Chancellor John McDonnell announced a Labour government would pilot schemes in the UK.

Proponents say that although it increases the total benefits spending by government, this is compensated for by savings made in administering the

---

118 A 2016 article in *The Economist*, of all places, concluded that GDP was "increasingly a poor measure of prosperity. It is not even a reliable gauge of production." www.economist.com/briefing/2016/04/30/the-trouble-with-gdp

119 It is fair to say that this approach in government and society is fairly revolutionary. For example, in May 2019, the New Zealand government announced its first ever wellbeing budget, a world-first, where spending decisions were based on improving wellbeing, not economic prosperity, GDP, employment or other more traditional economic measures.

120 This idea is not new, having been first described in Sir Thomas More's *Utopia* – in 1516!

welfare system (as claims no longer have to be evaluated or assessed). It also has long-term financial benefit in lessening societal problems associated with poverty (e.g. income and health inequality, and acquisitive crime).[121]

The only drawback? No one has (yet) advocated a plausible plan to make UBI affordable, even in relatively wealthy countries like the US. But if it were sufficiently funded (by a robot tax, for example) the implication for businesses would be to shift power from employer to employee – being without work would no longer carry the same financial and psychological burdens, as a job would no longer be essential.

Pilot UBI schemes are in place in Finland, amongst several other countries. In February 2019, the initial findings among 2,000 unemployed Finns put on UBI for two years were that they were not more likely to find work – but they were happier, healthier and less stressed.[122]

Losing work does not lead to bad decisions – but financial (and time) poverty does

A partial explanation of this effect can be found in behavioural science experiments that consistently show decision-making to be adversely affected by poverty. Making people financially better off can also benefit them in other ways. Financial stress makes it more difficult for people to think clearly, rationally and logically about important decisions, making it more likely for them to make their situation worse. Scarcity bias[123] also applies to time and money – the fewer of those resources we have, the more prone to cognitive biases we become.

"[T]here is emerging research which shows that financial worries absorb mental capacity – or 'bandwidth' – needed for attention and problem solving," said a 2016 report by the Behavioural Insights Team.

---

121   There is also a significant psychological benefit of not making people go through the indignity of attending job and disability assessment centres. Having seen these environments first hand in my work in the UK, they are often unpleasant experiences for all concerned – citizens understandably resent having to explain the circumstances of their unemployment or illness to a stranger, and staff are frequently harassed and threatened. Staff turnover is consequently high.

122   www.bbc.co.uk/news/world-europe-47169549

123   Part of our tendency towards loss aversion, explained on page 29.

One of their key recommendations for government was to remove administrative burden and increase cognitive ease, as in UBI schemes: "Policymakers should aim to minimise the time and mental costs of engaging in government services to make it easy for people on low incomes to make good decisions for themselves."[124]

The writer James Bloodworth, whom we shall hear more from in the next chapter, described the impact of working in an Amazon warehouse on his decision-making to me – a job where he was on a zero-hours contract, for minimum wage, in fairly appalling conditions.[125]

"When I was working for Amazon, I was walking around 10 miles a day. That was the average," says Bloodworth. "Doing all of this exercise, you would expect to be quite fit and healthy and to be losing weight. But actually I put on weight while I was doing the job. And I started smoking again … I also found I was drinking more … You finish work at close to midnight. And so you just go to McDonalds, you don't want to stand in the kitchen for an hour. The sorts of kitchens you're renting as well on that money … You're just getting McDonald's then you're getting up at 11 in the morning. Wolfing down whatever's there. And then going straight into work, long gaps between when you're eating, eating very high calorie food. The stress leads you to seek out things like chocolate, crisps and so on because it makes you feel better temporarily.

"When you're not deriving any pleasure from your work, you seek it out elsewhere."

In addition to poor decisions about health, anyone who has worked as a freelancer or contractor knows having regular income makes financial planning considerably easier. A payday loan with an APR of several thousand percent seems like an obviously terrible investment decision if you can afford to pay the rent. When that luxury is removed, it suddenly becomes more attractive. Businesses should consider the wider impact of staff not being able to make ends meet.

---

124 'Poverty and Decision-Making: How behavioural science can improve opportunity in the UK', Kizzy Gandy, Katy King, Pippa Streeter Hurle, Chloe Bustin and Kate Glazebrook, *The Behavioural Insights Team*, October 2016.

125 A zero-hours contract is one where no work is guaranteed – the employer can give as much or as little work to the employee as it wants (or needs). No certainty of work (or income) is provided. I interviewed Bloodworth for the ABP 'Psychology of Work' podcast.

Similarly, making people time scarce – by working consistently long hours for example – directly impacts decision-making and, ultimately, performance at work.[126]

As Kate Glazebrook, one of the authors of the BIT report, explained to me: "The mental processes that we undergo when we are poor, be that financially poor or time poor, actually have a lot of the same kinds of characteristics. If you think about somebody who's relatively wealthy, quite financially literate, might still be late on making payments on their credit cards. They literally don't have time, and they've got so many decisions they're taking in a given day, that they just don't quite get around to it even though rationally they absolutely should. Because the cost of not doing that is real."

She cites research by Eldar Shafir and Sendhil Mullainathan that found that being in a state of change from financial plenty to scarcity reduced the IQ level of the same Indian farmers from the top quartile to a median IQ, and from a median IQ to someone who was cognitively challenged. This was equivalent to the cognitive impairment that one might feel from losing a night of sleep.[127]

Critically, making your staff poor in time or money makes them less smart, and likely worse at their job. Any decisions a business makes that negatively impacts on the free time and financial security of your staff makes that business less smart too.

What behavioural science tells us about how we view work

Interestingly, UBI attracts criticism from those on the political left and right. The right because it rewards idleness or unwillingness to work, and the left because it puts no onus on business to address societal problems. Many also feel that it undervalues the importance of work for people as a marker of social status, giver of purpose and source of identity and meaning in our lives.

---

126   This is especially worrying when considering the impact of chronic under-funding creating excessive working hours for public sector workers, such as those in the NHS.
127   scholar.harvard.edu/files/sendhil/files/976.full_.pdf Much of this research is contained in their book, *Scarcity: Why Having Too Little Means So Much.*

These are primarily ideological issues. When it comes to the behavioural science, UBI presents an interesting solution. As we will see throughout this book, it subverts the traditional economic view of behaviour, and work in general – which is what behavioural science is all about.

The neoclassical economic viewpoint is that work is our means of acquiring resources (pay) to allow us to purchase goods and services, and to meet our hierarchy of needs. Even a basic understanding of human psychology shows us this is nonsense, as many of our needs are emotional, not financial. Additionally, the growing phenomenon of in-work poverty (for example, two-thirds of children in poverty in the UK live in a working family)[128] means this is also not true in economic terms. Solutions such as UBI could potentially lift people out of poverty, help them make better decisions, and free businesses to consider the most effective way to deliver goods and services – whether using humans or automation.

Leaving the humans free to focus on what they do best.

A *Fast Company* article about the future of work in 2100 predicted other business and societal changes unprecedented since the days of the Industrial Revolution:

> "[A]utomation will push future workers to roles and tasks that are quintessentially human, abolishing leftover vestiges of the industrial revolution – such as standardized working hours and traditional hierarchies – toward something that more resembles the tribal and community-oriented work structures of pre-industrial times."

Over the next 80 years, the changes suggested included ending the 9-to-5 workday in favour of a 30-hour working week, the destruction of traditional offices and hierarchies, and replacing the concept of retirement with regular working re-training breaks throughout a career.[129] Businesses that adopt test-tube behaviours to trial these new working structures can robustly evaluate if they can positively impact on productivity and wellbeing, and make the most of these wider societal and industrial changes.

Many businesses across the globe (including the financial services provider Simply Business in the UK) are now piloting four-day working weeks, for example. A trial by New Zealand company Perpetual Guardian in 2018 found this increased productivity, customer and staff engagement, reduced stress, and improved work-life balance. Revenue remained stable,

---

128   Joseph Rowntree Foundation.
129   www.fastcompany.com/90180181/this-is-what-work-will-look-like-in-2100

whilst costs went down, and the scheme was implemented permanently. Founder Andrew Barnes suggested it also helped address the gender pay gap and diversity in the workforce.

In the future, more automated, world of work, the remaining human jobs will have a more psychological foundation – so becoming a behavioural business is not just advantageous, but critical. For businesses to survive, and prosper, they need to consider not only which roles can be automated, but how they can make the remaining human roles motivating, rewarding and productive. If we are living in a world where working is less attractive – and possibly even unnecessary – then businesses that do not provide these roles will be unable to attract and retain human staff.

In the next chapter, we will discover what businesses can learn from behavioural science about providing good work – work that is rewarding, not just in financial terms – to generate the right behaviours from your human teams to make them happier, and more productive.

CHAPTER 14

The Science of Motivation – How to Provide Good Work and Nudge the Right Behaviours from Your Teams

What is good work?

I N HIS 2017 government-commissioned report, *Good Work,*[130] Matthew Taylor (chief executive of the RSA) sought to address challenges facing the current world of work. One was the increase in workers in the so-called 'gig economy' – that is, people who are not considered employees, often hired on zero-hours contracts (i.e. with no guarantee of work). Many of these jobs, such as working in Amazon warehouses, fast-food outlets, retail stores and behind the wheels of taxis, are the jobs most at risk of automation. Legislation seeking to provide more rights for these workers in terms of pay and leave was introduced in the UK in December 2018 as a direct result of this report.

The report also explicitly details what constitutes good work, and particularly the limits of financial incentives: "Pay is only one aspect in determining quality work; for many people fulfilment, personal development, work life balance or flexibility are just as important."

---

130 assets.publishing.service.gov.uk/government/uploads/system/uploads/attachment_data/
file/627671/good-work-taylor-review-modern-working-practices-rg.pdf

Matthew Taylor explained to me his view of what constitutes good work.[131]

"Work means different things to different people at different times," says Taylor. "You want a baseline of fairness and decent terms and conditions, then you want work that is flexible, so you can balance work and the rest of your life. You want to be part of a supportive team … You want a sense of purpose, you want to feel that what you're doing is useful and adding value. And you want some level of autonomy. You want to feel that you are trusted, that you're listened to, and are not just a cog in the machine."

Taylor concluded that it is incumbent on management in business to provide these conditions: "If you care about good work, as I do passionately, the one thing more above all else that you want to influence is the quality of management. And we need organisational forms that encourage better, more generous, more creative forms of management."

If you are in management you are also subconsciously role-modelling behaviours to others in your business.[132] Beyond not being an unethical or dishonest leader, this means better behaviours will also be encouraged amongst your teams – and so understanding and demonstrating these behaviours is essential to good leadership.

More money doesn't transform bad work into good work

James Bloodworth's sobering book, *Hired: Six Months Undercover in the Low Wage Economy*, details his experience working at Amazon as well as other low-paid, gig economy jobs, including driving for Uber, working in a call centre and as a carer. I interviewed Bloodworth about the working conditions he experienced at the Amazon Fulfilment Centre (FC) in Rugeley, Staffordshire.

"Everything centered in Amazon around productivity, and there was a huge turnover of staff," he said. "So people would be coming and going, there would be a new intake all the time of people, because everyone would just leave. And it was like a battery farm in a way … but for human beings."

---

131 I interviewed Matthew Taylor after his keynote speech at the 2018 ABP Conference, and the interview is available as an ABP podcast.
132 Simply by dint of your position, due to authority bias (explained on page 68).

Bloodworth quotes research from the GMB union that found that 91% of Amazon employees would not recommend it to others as a good place to work. He describes the ludicrously high turnover, punishment points issued for sick days, chronic late/under payment, and generally appalling working conditions. On one occasion he found a bottle of urine on a shelf – left there by a staff member unable to have a bathroom break and make his productivity targets.

"I set out to write a book about the low-paid economy," says Bloodworth. "And I thought it would largely revolve around material poverty. But most of the stuff that came up in Amazon was around the lack of autonomy, dignity, self-respect – you just didn't get those things from the job. And there was almost a sense of humiliation that kind of permeated the environment there. You were humiliated on a daily basis. Even wanting to use the toilet, you had to pass through security, and be admonished by security for having things in your pockets. You were treated as if you were in a very strict boarding school or in a police station or something. It was a very strange environment. And even if you made more money, it would still have been a fairly intolerable environment to work in."

Bloodworth's book, and the championing of it by US Senator Bernie Sanders and others as symptomatic of modern-day worker exploitation, was instrumental in Amazon's decision in October 2018 to increase the pay of all its workers. In the US, this rose to a minimum of $15 an hour, and in the UK to £9.50 (£10.50 in London) – a pay rise of at least 28% in London and 18% elsewhere.[133] Considering Amazon has so successfully used behavioural science to grow revenue from customers, this approach to improving staff motivation – pay people more to stop complaining – seems positively Neanderthal by comparison.

Doubly so, given the evidence from behavioural science is that money is a relatively ineffective motivator, overall. Although individual incentives can boost performance and productivity on average by up to 50%, it comes at a significant cost. Wharton Business School professors Adam Grant and Jitendra Singh say: "[f]inancial incentives, by definition, create inequalities in pay that often undermine performance, collaboration and retention … [T]he good results generated by financial incentives need to be weighed against the bad: encouraging unethical behaviour; creating pay inequality

---

133   www.theguardian.com/technology/2018/oct/02/amazon-raises-minimum-wage-us-uk-employees

that reduces performance and increases turnover; and decreasing intrinsic interest in the work."[134]

Even successful businesses like Amazon often seem to have a much poorer understanding of how to drive the right behaviours from their own staff – the people spending 40 hours a week (or more) on their premises – than their anonymous customers, whom they may engage with for a matter of seconds.

When considering what will keep the people in your business happy, behavioural science yet again tells us our intuitions are often erroneous. Compensation for our time in work – our pay – is only one part of the puzzle, and an incredibly ineffective tool for motivating. Our view of work is much more complex than that, and many more hidden, subconscious factors determine motivation and performance.

Bad work is bad for business

In psychological terms, as Taylor points out, there are subsistence levels of wellbeing that are necessary for jobs to be motivating. Professor Ivan Robertson is Emeritus Professor at the University of Manchester, and has published over 40 books on work and organisational psychology and nearly 200 scholarly articles/conference papers on wellbeing at work.

"It's simply the case that people whose wellbeing is higher are better employees," says Robertson. "They behave differently. They perform better. They're more collaborative with their colleagues. They're better with service users and customers, and so on. So the proposition that you should improve the wellbeing of your workforce for me is win-win for the organization and the individual. And it needs to be looked at as a strategic level thing that the organization should be doing, rather than simply saying 'we'll do this because it's nice for our employees'."[135]

A 2019 meta-analysis of over 300 different research studies including nearly 2m employees, by the Saïd Business School at Oxford University, concluded that there was a strong positive correlation between employee satisfaction with their company, productivity, and customer loyalty.

134 knowledge.wharton.upenn.edu/article/the-problem-with-financial-incentives-and-what-to-do-about-it/
135 I interviewed Professor Robertson with ABP board member Uzma Afridi at the 2018 ABP Conference for the ABP podcast.

Likewise, there was a strong negative correlation with staff turnover. They found that, ultimately, higher wellbeing at work led to greater profitability.[136]

Providing intrinsically motivating (i.e. good) work should therefore lead to happier, more productive employees, and is more effective in the long term for retention than extrinsic motivators (such as pay). In any case, there is nothing businesses can do to stop another business offering more money. Providing good work is something a business can control – the pay and conditions at competitors are not.

Speaking to James Bloodworth, it was clear that working in the gig economy did not provide good work in these terms. In the previous chapter, we heard about how working for Amazon led to Bloodworth making bad decisions. He also described how the long hours driving for Uber led to him and other drivers being dangerously unfit to drive at times. Because the productivity requirements in both those roles were determined by an anonymous algorithm, communicated via technology such as the Uber driver app, there was little to no emotional positivity or sense of meaning provided in those jobs.

One could argue that what the Uber management by algorithm model does provide is autonomy, and a feeling of being in control of your destiny. Lucy Standing is vice-chair of the Association for Business Psychology and a former head of graduate and global recruitment for companies such as JP Morgan, and sees some psychological positives in the gig economy model.

"Actually what I like about the gig economy and some of these platforms is the sense of autonomy and control that it gives people," says Standing. "Because if we visit some of the research and some of the literature around how people are most engaged, most satisfied at work, the overriding evidence seems to be that the people who can feel a sense of being in control are the people who have high levels of self-efficacy, which (for want of a better word) is just confidence. And these are the sorts of people that always report higher levels of satisfaction, and actually get promoted more than others.

"So anything that we can do to actually encourage people to feel responsible for their own destiny is far more the way that I would encourage organizations to go ... But at the heart of it is the more that an organization can drive people to feel more personally responsible for their actions, the better and happier those employees will be."

---

136   eureka.sbs.ox.ac.uk/7348/1/2019-04.pdf

Behavioural science tells us that a loss of autonomy – self-efficacy – is extremely damaging to motivation and wellbeing. According to Bloodworth, in the case of Amazon and Uber the autonomy provided to workers is illusory – the Uber driver app nudges them to drive on Friday and Saturday nights for the best fares, for example – and once that illusion is removed, it is psychologically harmful.

It is symptomatic of how businesses need to remember that, when dealing with human productivity, you are (metaphorically) feeding monkeys with cucumber and grapes – not simply programming an algorithm and setting it to "make people work harder".

Creating good habits at work

Behavioural science tells us that motivations are often irrational or counter-intuitive, so it can be effectively employed to encourage positive behaviours in the workplace – and stop negative ones. Laszlo Bock, former senior vice president of people operations at Google, says: "Nudges are an incredibly powerful mechanism for improving teams and organizations."[137]

One interesting example is "temptation bundling", which proves effective at getting people to complete necessary but boring tasks (such as administrative tasks, like timesheets) by coupling them with a pleasurable non-financial reward, rather than the threat of punishment. Our loss aversion bias motivates us to complete the task, lest we miss out on the fun.

Professor Katherine Milkman from the Wharton School at University of Pennsylvania conducted an experiment where participants were rewarded for attending a gym by getting chapters of audiobooks of popular novels such as *The Hunger Games* – increasing gym attendance by 51%.[138] An advertising agency in the US applied this principle, and installed a company beer tap that can only be used once staff completed their timesheets on a Friday – a far better incentive then the usual techniques of not paying outstanding expenses or locking people out of their email accounts.

When changing behaviour it is easier to break multiple bad habits at once, because once habits become ingrained they operate on a loop (see below). When a major change happens for a business (e.g. a restructure), this is the perfect time to instigate new processes and practices to encourage

---

137   In his book *Work Rules*.
138   pubsonline.informs.org/doi/abs/10.1287/mnsc.2013.1784

good habits. Working with a call centre, for example, our team instigated a range of nudges in the new environment following an office move. These included welfare initiatives, such as the introduction of adjustable desks to allow staff to stand or sit and healthy snacks, as well as environmental nudges to boost motivation, such as 3D-printed representations of each employee's financial goals (cars, houses etc.) to sit on their desks, and a change of wall colour to a shade of blue that aided concentration.

As a result of these low-cost nudges, after the office move staff wellbeing increased by 12% and retention by 80%, delivering over seven times the value of the investment in the project.

THE HABIT LOOP

The habit loop was described by American writer Charles Duhigg in his book, *The Power of Habit*, to explain how we create (and break) habits. Habits are hugely important as they form a large amount of our system-1, or automatic, behaviour, and consist of three elements: a cue; a routine; and a reward.

Example of a habit loop

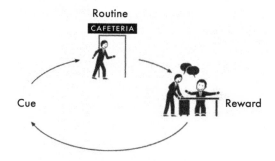

Source: *The Power of Habit*

In one example given by Duhigg, a cue (the time reaching 3:30pm) would activate his routine (going to the cafeteria to buy a chocolate cookie), which then triggered a reward of a chat with a colleague on his way back to his desk. The cue is a trigger that activates his automatic, system-1 processing mode, the routine is the behaviour itself, and the reward is the positive reinforcement of that behaviour – which can be purely emotional, as in this example.

This is in part based on research into the behaviour of rats in mazes, where researchers found that once rats discovered the best route they started using their *cerebral cortex* less (the part of the brain more involved in system-2 functions, like memory), and found more activity in the *basal ganglia* (more involved in system-1 decisions). Our habits have an evolutionary function allowing us to conserve energy – our Homer-like brains are essentially lazy and seek to avoid cognitive effort where possible, as we have seen elsewhere in this book.

The most useful aspect of this model is in identifying the most effective things to address to break or change a habit.[139] In Duhigg's case, to avoid eating a cookie every day, he kept the cue and reward the same but changed the routine to simply walking over to colleague's desk for a chat at 3:30pm. In the same way, the My QuitBuddy app described in part one gave smokers a different routine (opening and using the app) when triggered to smoke by the cue of the craving for nicotine – with the emotional reward of knowing they did not give in to temptation.

Creating better rewards can also reinforce a behaviour. Duhigg gives the example of Pepsadent toothpaste, who found that adding a minty fresh flavour to their toothpaste made the habit of brushing teeth stick. The flavour serves no purpose in terms of helping keep teeth clean, but consumers liked the emotional reward of the zingy clean feeling they got after brushing. Now most toothpaste brands do the same.

As we have seen elsewhere, cues, routines and rewards do not need to follow a rational view of human behaviour – in fact they often work better when they don't.

---

139   It is important to remember that habits are often difficult to build, and break. A 2010 study found that on average it took 66 consecutive days of doing something to create a consistent daily habit across a number of behaviours (Lally P, van Jaarsveld CHM, Potts HWW, Wardle J. 'How are habits formed: modelling habit formation in the real world', *Euro J Soc Psychol.* 2010;40:998–1009). But this varies between individuals and behaviours.

Think about your environment

Environmental nudges can be highly effective at boosting staff motivation and wellbeing – as in the call centre example, small changes can have surprisingly large effects. The evidence for office wall colour in particular is considerable. A 2018 systematic review found a significant influence of colour on affect (e.g. mood, emotion), wellbeing (e.g. stress, comfort), and performance (e.g. productivity, creativity).[140]

No one colour is best, as it is very dependent on the type of work and task. New-York-based Australian academic Adam Alter coined the term 'drunk tank pink' for a particular hue that has been effectively used by prisons and sports teams for its calming, testosterone-lowering effect. Norwich City Football Club painted their away dressing rooms in the colour for the 2018–19 season in the hope of affecting the performance of their opponents – correlation is not causation, but they won the division comfortably.[141]

In the same vein, referees in Australia's premier National Rugby League (NRL) competition complained that their pink shirts (changed to suit a corporate sponsor) undermined their authority to such a degree that they had to be changed. Colour matters – so remember that the next time you are considering new branding or a workplace makeover.[142]

Recent research also shows the modern norm of open-plan offices may not promote collaboration, interaction and productivity, as previously assumed. The noise, distraction and lack of privacy meant that in one study of 16,000 people in a Chinese call centre, those working from home were actually 13% more productive, happier and less likely to leave, than colleagues in an open plan office.[143] In another, face-to-face communication actually decreased by 70% after two Fortune 500 companies moved from

---

140 ajbes.e-iph.co.uk/index.php/ajbes/article/view/152/pdf

141 Writing as a lifelong fan of their bitter rivals, Ipswich Town, I was hugely disappointed by the success of this particular experiment, and found it deeply painful to include here. But integrity won out.

142 I asked Alter on Twitter about this particular case. "There might be something in it," was his reply.

143 www.nber.org/papers/w18871 This certainly accords with my own experience. My working regimen combines office and home-based working, and when completing what Cal Newport calls 'deep work' (i.e. tasks requiring concentration and system-2 effort), I am much more productive at home. For more collaborative, less intensive, work, I am much more effective in the office.

cubicles to open-plan (whilst virtual communication, such as emails, increased).[144]

My colleague Koen Smets has over 20 years experience as an organisation development professional and consultant, 'accidental' behavioural economist and prolific writer on the application of behavioural science in management. He argues this kind of intervention is under-used.

"I think organisational life seems to be the last bastion of *homo economicus*," says Smets. "The tendency in organisations is still very much towards using incentives as instruments to get people to do something, rather than use a nudge, like changing defaults ... The open plan office is a nice example of an externality, somebody says: 'Okay, we can save some money.' And they haven't thought about the impact on productivity."

Normalising good behaviour and providing positive motivation

These kinds of nudges can incrementally influence individual behaviour, but, to become effective, businesses need good behaviours to become the norm across teams. To succeed, a business needs to provide and encourage good work for all, not some. Behavioural science can also help here.

Research into social norms demonstrates that making positive behaviours more salient than bad ones can help normalise those behaviours. Highlighting a bad behaviour (through a company-wide, 'don't do this' email, for example) could have the unintended effect of making it seem common. Instead, businesses should make the focus the majority who are exhibiting the desired behaviour, and frame it positively, e.g. "99% of staff submit their expenses on time."[145]

Codes of conduct and agreed shared values for your business, which team members have to actively commit to (by signing a declaration, for example), are a great way of normalising behaviour.[146] Reminding people of these values at the relevant times, such as before completing key forms or prior to meetings, and having customer service charters (for example)

---

144 royalsocietypublishing.org/doi/full/10.1098/rstb.2017.0239
145 See the explanation of social norms on page 10.
146 Because of post-rationalisation, explained on page 154.

prominently displayed in the workplace, are effective, environmental nudges to good behaviour.[147]

We've already seen that money is a fairly poor motivator and encourages selfish behaviour. But there are creative ways to use financial incentives to normalise positive behaviour, and increase wellbeing and productivity. One solution Wharton Business School professors Adam Grant and Jitendra Singh suggest is to pay people based on the inputs, not outputs, of their work. This is because we are more motivated by intrinsic, not extrinsic, rewards.[148]

For example, if a company has a good year, then you may think it is right to reward all staff accordingly. But a bonus based on company profitability is often difficult to relate to your specific contribution, unless you are the CEO. Instead, a bonus because you personally helped produce more widgets this month than last is more motivating, since it is more salient and within your control – even if the company ultimately sold them at a loss (or not at all). As Lucy Standing pointed out earlier, you will have more confidence (self-efficacy) in achieving this goal.

The US online shoe manufacturer Zappos (now part of Amazon) introduced a novel approach to using cash incentives for staff retention. On completion of a successful probation period staff were not offered a bonus by way of a 'golden hello' – they were instead offered a substantial sum of money ($1,000) to *leave*. Amazon has now extended the same scheme to its full-time FC workers, offering up to $5,000 every year for them to leave on agreement that they can never work for Amazon again.

The logic is that for an employee to turn down that money, they must really want to work there – and if they have any doubts, that will create dissonance.[149] From Amazon's point of view, it saves money in the long term that would have gone on wages, training, and overheads on someone who ultimately is likely to leave, or on a new employee. As a way to use

---

147 These are examples of priming effects, where environmental, contextual factors can have a subconscious effect on subsequent behaviour.
148 Grant and Singh. The risk here is that people can be motivated to then achieve personal goals to the detriment of collective/business goals, for example, by becoming over-competitive and sabotaging others' work. Adam Grant's work describes this is a marker of a taker (someone who extracts more personal value than they put into a business – the opposite of a giver), and can be avoided by making intrinsic rewards collective (i.e. for a group) rather than an individual. And by focusing on recruiting givers rather than takers.
149 An example of post-rationalisation, explained on page 154.

financial incentives to positively change behaviour it is counter-intuitive – and ingenious.

This is another example of how behavioural science tells us that motivation is a fickle beast, and simply paying people more is a very blunt tool to apply. The best metaphor I can think of is the wind – some days it is stronger than others, and some places (like individuals) get blown about more than others. Businesses that identify those times and places where it blows strongest, and verify it through testing (i.e. adopting a test-tube approach), can make best use of it – and even give it a bit of a boost when required. Those businesses can then provide good work, and ensure that positive behaviours become the norm within the organisation.

Of course, one of the best ways to ensure motivated and productive teams is to hire the most capable people for the job – and then assess (and reward) their performance accordingly. Again, there is much that behavioural science can tell us about this, and we shall explore this next.

CHAPTER 15

Building Effective Teams Using Behavioural Science – Finding and Maintaining Success

Recruitment: the traditional home of psychology in business

I N PART ONE, we heard how pioneering behavioural economist Daniel Kahneman trained as an occupational psychologist, designing better processes to recruit and assess pilots for the Israeli Air Force.

This heritage of identifying people capable of pulling a trigger – without it causing them lasting psychological trauma – has led to a focus of psychology in business on recruitment, assessment and performance.

Non-military employers soon realised that they could also better predict success of recruits in (slightly) less stressful circumstances by using statistically validated surveys (psychometric tests), and that business psychologists could help them in assessing performance, motivation, wellbeing and diversity. Industrial-organisational psychology (I-O psychology) has become a well-established academic discipline, a major industry and the most common role taken by psychologists in business.

Ben Williams,[150] founder of assessment design firm Sten10, is one of the leading experts in the use of tests for recruitment and assessment in the UK. He described to me the capabilities of these kinds of tools for business in terms of measuring behaviour, motivation, knowledge, personality and reasoning – and how, despite being well-established, they are infrequently employed, especially when recruiting at senior levels. Too few businesses are using these established techniques, and letting biases and heuristics prevent them from recruiting the best people.

"I think the issue with our profession is that it does have its roots in an academic setting," says Williams. "There are industries that tend to rebel against this type of structured psychological assessment. One of them would be the creative industry ... the very concept of creativity is notoriously controversial to try to measure, but also just any aspect of people's performance in a creative industry is tough ... In entrepreneurial firms, again, a lot of the hire will be based upon convenience or initial enthusiasm, and it's an expense that perhaps they hadn't been banking upon – putting someone through a rigorous assessment."[151]

Recruiting the right people for the right reasons

The reason for adopting scientifically verified testing methods in business (even more creative or entrepreneurial enterprises) is that the very nature of an assessment or interview can disadvantage some, and (unconscious) biases of the recruiter can creep into the test itself. Using insights from behavioural science ensures the biases inherent in certain tests do not disadvantage people based on irrelevant criteria that have nothing to do with their ability to do the job.

---

150   In addition, Williams is also the chair of the Association for Business Psychology, and an associate fellow of the British Psychological Society.

151   As an example of this, at no stage of my career have I ever completed any form of psychometric test before being offered a job. No agency in the advertising, marketing or media world that I know of used them, and the only test I was ever given was a simple number reasoning test for my very first graduate job in media (described in part six). This test seemed entirely pointless because all my subsequent calculations in the job were done in Microsoft Excel, but I guess it may have served a purpose in validating that the Maths A-Level on my CV wasn't made up.

This is borne out by research from the web-based recruitment platform Applied, whose CEO and co-founder is Kate Glazebrook, formerly of the BIT.

"We use behavioural science and data science to improve quality of recruitment decisions," says Glazebrook. "So not only making them less biased, but also trying to improve the predictive validity of those decisions."

As part of this approach, the platform does away with CVs altogether, favouring assessments that relate to the specific requirements of the role. "We've seen by reshaping what you see, and how, is that over half of the candidates hired through our platform wouldn't otherwise be hired," says Glazebrook. "So under a traditional CV sifting process these candidates would be put in the 'no' pile, even though they demonstrably have the skills that you're looking for, for the job. And statistically they are much more likely to come from more diverse backgrounds."

As we saw with Amazon's recruiting AI, which instantly screened out all female CVs, if you design an algorithm – or a recruitment process – that reflects the biases of the recruiter then these will be magnified. The writer Caroline Criado Perez showed in her book, *Invisible Women: Exposing Data Bias in a World Designed for Men,* that data biases against women exist throughout the workplace – from gender biased language in recruitment ads, to the default temperature that office air cons are set at being based on the male metabolism and therefore too cold for most women. These (unconscious) biases will also inhibit the ability to recruit based on ability unless businesses design them out – we heard in the last part how using the Applied platform increased the proportion of female applicants to tech jobs by 25–30%.

Harvard professor and behavioural economist Iris Bohnet says in her book, *What Works: Gender Equality by Design,* that "Replacing intuition, informal networks, and traditional rules of thumb with quantifiable data and rigorous analysis is a first step toward overcoming gender bias."

Similarly, social psychology research has identified that those from higher social status and income backgrounds have greater self-efficacy and therefore (over-)confidence in their ability to perform a role during an assessment. This gives them an inherent advantage before they even enter the room, and a 25% greater chance of being in a high-earning job.[152]

---

152 'The psychology of social class: How socioeconomic status impacts thought, feelings, and behaviour', Antony S. R. Manstead, *British Journal of Social Psychology* (2018), and 'A Winning Personality: the effects of background on personality and earnings', Dr R de Vries and Dr J Rentfrow, Sutton Trust (2016).

Privilege begets privilege – at the expense of ability. External expertise, behavioural science-based tools like Applied, and the use of professional business psychologists, to design recruitment and assessment processes that make effective use of evidence to remove these biases is critical to recruiting for the right reasons.[153]

The other reason bias in recruitment is bad is that even less obviously troubling biases, as we have seen, can still be totally irrational. They are often wholly superficial and incredibly poor at predicting people's ability to do a job. Evidence suggests that people often make hiring decisions in the first 20 seconds of an interview. There is also evidence that we generally think people who wear glasses are more intelligent, that more attractive people are less intelligent, and that people with a Midlands accent are less intelligent than Scots.

So good luck finding work if you are a Brummie model with 20/20 vision.

"If I wanted to most succeed in an interview I should mimic the regional accent of the interviewer, to construct that 'similar to me effect'," says Lucy Standing. "If you asked the interviewer why they hired them, they would post-rationalise the reason as being most comfortable with that person, for example. A bias is not always something that people would be cognisant of, but because it has been observed it is something that rightly concerns us in designing assessments. Now we can use AI to assess keywords, tone of voice, hesitation, to assess confidence and knowledge and remove the guesswork in a more rational, observed manner."

As we saw with other business decisions in the last part of the book, removing bias and noise through new technology and unbiased data can increase your odds of hiring the right person for the job. It can also make the recruitment process much more efficient.

"What we discovered is that if you add up all of the time you would have needed to look at about three times as many CVs to get the same number of high-quality candidates [as found by using Applied]," says Kate

---

153   Ben Williams and I have a shared experience that he uses as a prime example of unconscious bias in selection: the Oxbridge application process. As non-public school educated 17-year-old boys who grew up in small provincial towns (Woking and Ipswich respectively), turning up for interview in a Tudor cloistered court by a tweed-wearing don was hugely intimidating, and completely alien to us both. Had we attended Harrow or Eton... probably not so much. I should point out it didn't necessarily unduly disadvantage us both, as we both got in (Oxford in Ben's case, Cambridge in mine). We both partly attribute this to having interviewers who were relatively young and did not wear tweed, which put us much more at ease.

Glazebrook. "Which translates into considerable savings in terms of time ... What we've been doing is actually bringing to the first stage better predictors of talent, which means that every stage that comes thereafter is significantly more likely to be a fit for a candidate. Some of our clients have been hiring two to three times more candidates off the same hiring process than they were before ... What we're also seeing is some of our clients are able to drop whole stages of the recruitment process, because we also work with them to prove the predictive validity of every stage ... And that means you can save hours in recruiters time that's often spent garnering just a little bit more information."

Assessing potential and predicting success

Concentrating on the data and characteristics that make people good at their job – and ignoring everything else – means businesses also become much better at assessing potential performance. The world of sport, for example, has been completely transformed by how data is now used to assess and predict future performance, removing the biases of scouts and coaches from the process, and minimising the risk involved in acquiring players (often for millions of pounds). In sport, where competitive advantage (winning) is all that counts, this has delivered tangible – and remarkable – results.[154]

In 2012, I presented at a government communications conference in Canberra, where the keynote speaker was *Nudge* co-author and Harvard professor Cass Sunstein. To illustrate the huge efficiencies that nudge policies were delivering to the US Government, Sunstein used an analogy from the movie *Moneyball*. Based on Michael Lewis's brilliant account of how the Oakland Athletic's Major League Baseball team massively over-

---

154 Worth also noting the huge impact that sports psychologists have had in performance across the board. The England football team, for example, have been transformed since they employed a manager (Gareth Southgate) who reportedly cares as much about the wellbeing of his players as their performance on the pitch, and employs qualified psychologists as part of his team. The team even used psychometric testing to ascertain the most suitable players to take penalty kicks, thereby overcoming their unenviable record of never winning a World Cup shoot-out on their way to the semi-final in 2018. With the greatest respect to Eric Dier, I, like many other England fans, was somewhat surprised to see him take the most critical spot kicks based on his ability relative to the rest of the team. But he was cool as a cucumber under the immense pressure – and even repeated the feat in the 2019 Euro Nations League. His lucrative Pizza Hut advertising contract remains on hold.

achieved in the early years of the century, the book and movie describe how they remained competitive despite having the lowest wage budgets in the league.

Sunstein's slide was titled, 'Evidence, Not Intuitions'. He quoted a passage in the book where Oakland General Manager Billy Beane is challenging his scouts on their choice of players to acquire – in this case, a good hitter.[155]

"'My only question,' says Billy, 'if he's that good a hitter why doesn't he hit better?'

"Over and over the old scouts will say, 'The guy has a great body,' or 'This guy may be the best body in the draft.' And every time they do, Billy will say, 'We're not selling jeans here,' and deposit yet another highly touted player, beloved by the scouts, onto his [bad] list.'" [156]

The biases of scouts, just like recruiters in business, were so ingrained, that their focus was on irrelevant criteria (physical attributes) rather than *whether they could actually hit a ball*.[157] Using the skills of Paul DePodesta, a Harvard economics graduate and data whizz, Beane was able to exploit the irrationalities of the market to acquire under-valued (and unconventional) players and gain competitive advantage.

This approach has now been replicated across the world in different sports. Liverpool Football Club's 2019 Champions League victory can to some extent be traced to the use of sophisticated analytics – their director of research, Ian Graham, had been instrumental in the decision to hire mercurial manager Jurgen Klopp and star players like Mo Salah and Phillippe Coutinho.[158]

These examples are illustrative of how to predict and measure success in business, as well as sport. Use (unbiased) evidence, not intuition. Focus

---

155 Beane is very much the hero of the story – the part played by Brad Pitt in the movie.

156 *Moneyball,* Lewis M., Norton (2003).

157 This is not just true of baseball. Such is the strength of these biases that seemingly obvious talent can be over-looked in any field. By the age of 25 Tottenham Hotspur and England international footballer Harry Kane had already won a golden boot for scoring the most goals at the 2018 World Cup; been top goalscorer in the Premier League twice; achieved the record for most Premier League players of the month awards; and had the best strike rate (0.7 goals per game) in Premier League history. Yet as a young player he was rejected by Arsenal (who thought him "a bit chubby" and "not very athletic"), Spurs and Watford, before Spurs gave him a second chance. As journalist Jim White noted: "The reason he did not initially turn heads in the academy system was that he wasn't big and he wasn't particularly quick, the two attributes much valued in youth development."

158 www.nytimes.com/2019/05/22/magazine/soccer-data-liverpool.html

on the right metrics – and ignore everything else. Embrace diversity, don't fear it.

Lucy Standing says: "In the case of recruitment, we have been recruiting incredibly badly for a very, very long period of time. The best we can hope for, using the best methods available, is to predict success about a third of the time. And that is because the person best placed to predict success is the person doing the job – who very often is not the person doing the recruiting."

Standing also points out that the traditional approach to hiring (interviews) creates completely the wrong expectations, and is a poor predictor: "You typically wouldn't marry someone without dating them first. You wouldn't buy a house without seeing it first. People are expected to walk into jobs after meeting the person who isn't doing the job, and consequently will often feel they have been mis-sold or given the wrong expectations. That can be changed through internships, apprenticeships, and changing our focus of all our attention away from recruiting people at 18 or 21, or graduates. If we look at population trends, all the growth is coming from ageing – recruitment is ripe for significant change, and psychology can do a wonderful job in helping to guide that."

When our ability to predict what makes a good recruit is so poor, and the costs involved in making a bad hire are so high,[159] surely we should be using every possible tool in our arsenal to increase our chances of success? And sciencing the shit out of recruitment too?

Test-tube recruiting

Speak to a business psychologist and often the conversation will get into technical terminology like face validity, selection methods and reliability. Aside from demonstrating expertise, this is because *there is a lot of bad science out there.*

The growth of jobs like life coach and wellbeing advisor means that, understandably, those who have qualifications and expertise want to

---

159 We saw in the previous chapter that one reason why businesses such as Amazon seem to be embracing the associate model, rather than employing people on a full-time basis, is so that they can hire and fire at will with minimal cost implications. One could hypothesise that this approach also allows them to weed out any bad recruits simply by a process of elimination. Aside from the troubling ethical questions this raises, and governments are legislating to prevent them doing this, it is a wholly inefficient way to recruit compared to simply designing a better recruitment process in the first place.

differentiate themselves from those who do not (as a GP distances themselves from a homeopath). Tools such as the Myers-Briggs Type Indicator (MBTI), which groups people into archetypes such as whether they are more or less intuitive (i.e. 'thinking' or 'feeling'), persist in being used by businesses despite having their validity questioned for many years.

I was fortunate to have the opportunity to speak to Professor Peter Saville,[160] a pioneering figure in the world of assessment and often credited with establishing the modern industry of occupational psychometrics. Saville co-founded the company SHL in his garage – which was later listed on the London Stock Exchange for £240m. The *World Anthology of Psychology* describes Saville as "one of the most influential psychologists of our time".

"The original Myers Briggs used to say on the answer sheet profile chart: 'If you don't like the type then choose one you do'," says Saville. "It was designed as an educational testing service by Myers and Briggs for providing careers advice for college students. But everybody's walking around saying: 'I'm INTJ, I am this, I am that.' ... Even if it's used in careers guidance I still feel that you ought to have some construct and empirical validity for that instrument. Otherwise we might as well use horoscopes ... I'm not a great lover of 'types' [in general]. The problem is that when you take some type instruments, if you retest people the same day the results change."

Using something more than human intuition and guesswork, and its concomitant biases, is better than nothing – Saville says there is good evidence that getting people to choose their type actually works quite well. But, if a business wants to embed test-tube behaviours, then using evidenced techniques and data, and removing biases from the process to test and learn in recruitment, leads to much better outcomes for everyone involved.

Training is not enough

Simply making people aware of unconscious biases does not remove them from the process, if their behaviour remains unchanged. Not only does this prevent you hiring the right people, it is dangerous – if a business's hiring policy (as with Amazon's AI) has an inherent bias, then you are breaking the law if it is demonstrable you were hiring or not hiring someone for these reasons – conscious or not.

---

160   I interviewed Professor Peter Saville for a podcast with ABP board member Gab Galassi after his keynote at the 2018 ABP conference.

"It's estimated that in the United States about $8bn is spent every year just by US corporates on some version of unconscious bias or diversity training," says Kate Glazebrook. "Unconscious bias and diversity training tends to do a pretty good job of raising awareness and engagement with the issues, which is really important. Unfortunately, when they've tested the impact on actual decisions, whether you make a slightly different decision three months later than you otherwise would, they haven't shown much evidence that it actually affects behaviour … I think we're expecting too much from training. By definition, these unconscious biases are unconscious … What we should be thinking about is pairing that awareness with tools that help us to make the best decisions we can make in our everyday lives."[161]

Embedding these tools into recruitment processes is provably much more effective than training alone. In one famous experiment, a symphony orchestra found that introducing blind auditions increased the likelihood that a female musician would advance by 50%, and substantially increased the proportion of women hired.[162] In France, screening of CVs must be done blind (i.e. with names and ages removed) for this reason, and to prevent bias on the basis of ethnicity. Words and language carry subconscious meaning, and affect behaviour accordingly.

"One of the things we do as part of the tool is we highlight every time you use a word, and provide ungendered synonyms," says Glazebrook. "So you can think about ways of making sure that you're not inadvertently skewing your applicant pool by particular gender. There is also evidence that suggests that having a very long list of job requirements can inadvertently also shape who applies to the job. They've tended to find that women, for

161   A 2018 report by the Equality and Human Rights Commission looking at the evidence on effectiveness of unconscious bias training (UBT) concluded: "The evidence for UBT's ability effectively to change behaviour is limited … There is potential for back-firing effects when UBT participants are exposed to information that suggests stereotypes and biases are unchangeable." warwick.ac.uk/services/ldc/researchers/resource_bank/unconscious_bias/ub_an_assessment_of_evidence_for_effectiveness.pdf

162   Claudia Goldin and Cecilia Rouse, 'Orchestrating Impartiality: The Impact of 'Blind' Auditions on Female Musicians', *American Economic Review* 90 (2000): 715–741. Interestingly, to make these auditions truly blind, it was necessary not only to erect a screen between the assessors and the musicians but also to ask the musicians to remove their shoes – apparently the sound of the musician's shoes on the hardwood floor as they walked on stage gave clues to their gender. I often wonder whether these experiments provided inspiration to the format adopted by popular TV talent show, *The Voice*, where the celebrity judges have their backs turned to the wannabe singers, only getting to see them once convinced of their singing ability. Part of the appeal of the show is (I think) seeing the judges' preconceptions and biases challenged in this way.

example, are a bit less likely to apply to a job where there's a very long list of job requirements. Or rather, that women tend to prefer to have 90% plus of those job requirements before they're willing to throw their hat in the ring. Whereas men might be more willing to do it at about 60%."[163]

Diversity is good for business

Aside from the moral hazard involved in letting bias creep into your recruitment and assessment processes, the lack of diversity that can result is simply bad for business.

There is mounting evidence that more diverse teams are simply *better at the job*. In particular, having a diversity of viewpoints and opinions – cognitive diversity – leads to more questioning of conventional wisdom, less confirmation bias (see below), and therefore a more experimental, growth mindset. As we saw in part one, developing these test-tube behaviours is critical to successfully understanding and applying behavioural science, and so embedding these behaviours in your teams can drive business success.

Building a team of 'yes men' (and in many cases they will almost certainly be men) will be more likely to stifle creativity, create a culture of defensive decision-making and limit experimentation. A more diverse team – in thoughts, background and approaches – is more likely to generate the kind of counter-intuitive solutions that recognise the irrationalities of human behaviour.

A McKinsey study in 2015, titled 'Diversity Matters', examined data for 366 public companies across a range of industries in Canada, Latin America, the United Kingdom, and the United States. It found that companies in the top quartile for racial and ethnic diversity are 35% more likely to have financial returns above their respective national industry medians, and companies in the top quartile for gender diversity are 15% more likely.

Not only does diversity benefit the bottom line, it can also – counter-intuitively – lead to more harmony, empathy and wellbeing amongst teams, and increase retention.

---

163 Contrary to popular belief, Glazebrook says this is not purely due to a confidence gap between men and women: "It's perhaps the case that women believe that if you've listed out 10 different requirements of the job that they are in fact requirements. And that if you don't have them, then that might be an impediment to being successful. Whereas men may be more likely to read those 10 requirements as the sort of 'purple unicorn' that the organization would love to have, but most people know no one's going to meet them."

"We are more likely to like people who are like ourselves," says Ben Williams. "That, of course, could then lead to a lack of diversity within teams. And that person who doesn't go out after work for a drink or a catch up with the rest of the team, because of either family commitments or religious observances, may then fail to fit in as well, and may decide to leave."

CONFIRMATION BIAS

In 1951, an American Football match took place between Dartmouth and Princeton university teams. Due to the long-standing rivalry between the two sides, it was a notoriously violent match – the quarterbacks for both teams were hospitalised.

Afterwards, a couple of psychology professors called Hastorf and Cantril decided to see how opinions between fans of the two teams varied about the match. They showed 324 fans (of both sides) footage of the game, and asked them to count how many fouls each team committed. Princeton fans 'saw' twice as many fouls committed by Dartmouth players as the Dartmouth fans did.

They concluded: "The game 'exists' for a person and is experienced by him only insofar as certain happenings have significances in terms of his purpose." Without getting too philosophical, the implication is that we experience events through the subconscious lens of our own assumptions, beliefs and social associations.

This is one of the most famous experiments identifying the tendency or predisposition by which we tend to give more weight, or search for, information that confirms our existing beliefs: known as confirmation bias. Sport is merely one of the most obvious manifestations. If a referee gives a contentious decision against our team, they are biased against us – if they give a favourable one, they are a good referee.

In recent years, social media has given a whole new dimension to this effect. We create intellectual/filter bubbles through our choice of friends or followers. We connect more with people who share similar views to us, and thus we are only shown information that accords with our pre-existing views.

This has the effect of filtering out diverse viewpoints, meaning that our decision-making may not be fully informed by the wealth of options and opinions out there, and our views become more entrenched. It has been argued that it makes reasoned political debate impossible and has led to the increase in populist movements around the globe, by reinforcing existing prejudices.

A related consequence of confirmation bias is the sunk-cost fallacy (also known as escalation of commitment): the belief in maintaining a course of action because of previously committed expense or resources, despite evidence that it would be wrong to continue.[164] In a meeting, this might be encapsulated in a phrase like: 'this is how we've always done things here', or, 'it's too late to change our minds now'. Colloquially, we refer to it as 'throwing good money after bad'.

In business, confirmation bias can manifest in the prioritisation of information or data that confirms an existing course of action or belief (and de-prioritisation of better evidence or views to the contrary). This can actively prevent innovation, experimentation and the development of new insight – and is characteristic of a fixed mindset rather than a growth mindset.

I vividly remember once encountering this when I worked at the Department of Health. In a 2007 meeting, I suggested testing a new course of action to one of the other campaign teams.

A colleague (who had been working in the same role for 30 years) gave the somewhat testy reply: "We tried that in 1982. It didn't work."

Generating psychological safety

Charles Duhigg, author of *The Power of Habit* and *Smarter, Faster, Better: How to be Productive*, investigated a Google project – code-named 'Aristotle' – that looked at data on hundreds of Google's teams to figure out why some stumbled while others soared. Google had been blindly applying

---

164 At the time of writing (early 2019), the UK government's Brexit policy is fast becoming the new textbook example of this, replacing the oft-cited example of US government policy during the Vietnam war.

conventional wisdom (such as it is better to put introverts together) without validation, and wanted to move away from assessing individual performance to look at what is critical to success for teams. As Duhigg puts it: "If a company wants to outstrip its competitors, it needs to influence not only how people work but also how they work together."

Google's people operations department looked at everything from how frequently particular people ate together, to which traits the best managers shared. They found two behaviours were shared by good teams: members spoke in roughly the same proportion ('conversational turn-taking'); and were skilled at intuiting the feelings of other team members (i.e. empathy). These contribute to a higher overall intelligence and performance of a group, and were more important than intelligence of individual team members.[165]

These behaviours are reflective of what is known as psychological safety – a group culture that the Harvard Business School professor Amy Edmondson defines as a "shared belief held by members of a team that the team is safe for interpersonal risk-taking." Psychological safety is "a sense of confidence that the team will not embarrass, reject or punish someone for speaking up," Edmondson wrote in a study published in 1999. "It describes a team climate characterized by interpersonal trust and mutual respect in which people are comfortable being themselves."[166]

In short: celebrating and encouraging cognitive diversity. Google's data indicated that psychological safety, more than anything else, was critical to making a team work.

Psychological safety is also critical to a growth mindset and embedding test-tube behaviours in business. Without the freedom to fail, and create counter-intuitive, occasionally wacky ideas (which behavioural science often gives us), you cannot generate hypotheses for testing. Science needs to be fuelled by creativity to generate new hypotheses, and this is enhanced by cognitive diversity and psychological safety. Otherwise a business will just be testing the same things over and over again – and the same things their competitors are.

When I was leading communications strategy for the Australian Federal Government, I instigated a weekly brainstorm for anyone on the

---

165 Interestingly the social status research quoted above also found that lower socio-economic status (SES) people tend to be more empathic, and show more active listening behaviours. So one could hypothesise that these norms would be more natural in teams of individuals from lower SES backgrounds.

166 web.mit.edu/curhan/www/docs/Articles/15341_Readings/Group_Performance/Edmondson%20Psychological%20safety.pdf

team (at all levels) to attend – with mandatory attendance at least once a month.[167] Although our workforce was not the most age diverse (I was one of the oldest at 34 years old), we reflected Sydney's (and Australia's) diverse ethnography, with 17 different nationalities represented amongst the 30-odd employees.[168]

There were simple rules for these sessions that ensured conversational turn-taking and empathy, both important for any effective ideation session. What made this initiative particularly effective was the diversity of opinions and ideas, the volume of innovative outputs, and the culture of psychological safety it created. It had a noticeable effect on team bonding, liking for colleagues, and collaboration.[169] The importance of these became such that, irrespective of other pressures, we ensured these happened every week without fail – and other teams copied the approach.[170] The award-winning XTL campaign described in part two was created directly as a result of one of these brainstorms.

By contrast, without this diversity and psychological safety, working with people who think and act the same way exposes the same biases and generates a consensus effect – an assumption that everyone thinks the same way. In part six, we shall see how damaging this consensus effect has been to the marketing industry, as an example.

As Duhigg puts it: "[t]he paradox, of course, is that Google's intense data collection and number crunching have led it to the same conclusions that good managers have always known. In the best teams, members listen to one another and show sensitivity to feelings and needs … Project Aristotle is a reminder that when companies try to optimize everything, it's sometimes easy to forget that success is often built on experiences – like emotional interactions and complicated conversations and discussions of

---

167 There was also a not-so-subtle incentive for people to attend – my wife used to bake a delicious cake for the meeting each week.

168 My brilliant friend and colleague Thang Ngo, head of Australia's largest multicultural marketing agency, found this out and was instrumental in ensuring this diversity was maintained. According to 2016 data, 29% of the Australian population were born overseas (Australian Bureau of Statistics).

169 We were undoubtedly also helped by the sheer variety of briefs that working for government creates. One week the challenge might be climate change, the next taxation, the next road safety – all topics that people might not otherwise get to work on.

170 They remained in place after I left, run by my then junior Chris Colter – now the national strategy director for Initiative Australia.

who we want to be and how our teammates make us feel – that can't really be optimized." [171]

Understanding behaviour is critical to effective recruitment, assessment and performance because these are business issues that relate to people, with their concomitant biases and emotions.

And people are not productivity-driven, uber-rational robots.

---

171   Quotes are taken from Duhigg's *New York Times* article about this project, itself adapted from his book *Smarter, Faster, Better.* www.nytimes.com/2016/02/28/magazine/what-google-learned-from-its-quest-to-build-the-perfect-team.html?module=inline

CHAPTER 16
Behavioural Science
in the Workplace
WHAT TO DO NOW

I N THIS PART, we have seen how behavioural science helps businesses understand how to get the best from the humans in their business. It enables them to address the challenges of increasing automation, providing good (motivating and rewarding) work, encouraging positive behaviours from teams, and recruiting and assessing performance more effectively, by:

- demonstrating that the jobs least likely to be automated will have a stronger psychological foundation;

- helping define what constitutes good (i.e. intrinsically motivating) work, because good pay is not sufficient to compensate for bad conditions – and work may not even be necessary for people to work to survive and be happy in the future;

- understanding that bad work – that is poorly paid, demanding in terms of time, or negatively impacts wellbeing – also negatively affects performance in the role, retention and ultimately profitability;

- demonstrating that autonomy, social norms and environmental factors have a more significant impact on motivation and performance than money alone;

- showing that recruitment and assessment processes, that rely on unvalidated techniques or training only, often result in hiring or assessing people based on irrelevant criteria due to our behavioural biases.

For businesses that wish to make effective use of behavioural science in the workplace to succeed and grow, it is essential to embed test-tube behaviours internally to find what works in terms of recruitment and assessment, rewarding and motivating staff, and designing the most effective workplace and conditions, by:

- recognising that it is incumbent on management to provide good work, and to role model positive behaviours;

- ensuring objective, validated methods and tools are used to recruit;

- enabling better prediction of future success when recruiting and assessing through using unbiased data, rigorous processes and embracing diversity;

- using financial incentives carefully and creatively (e.g. using collective incentives, not individual), and providing workplaces that encourage autonomy, positive social interactions and desirable workplace behaviours;

- embedding psychological safety and cognitive diversity to fuel creativity and innovation through fairer recruitment, and by enabling test-tube behaviours.

PART
FIVE

Behavioural Science and Your Customers

CHAPTER 17

The Dangers of Post-rationalisation – How Behavioural Science Demonstrates That Much Market Research is Flawed

The Oval Office and the Press Office

T HE PEOPLE WORKING in your business are not Spock (or a robot), and neither are your customers. Behavioural science helps businesses better understand how, and why, people buy your products or services, because purchasing behaviour can be just as irrational as in other areas of business.

When developing anti-smoking campaigns for government in the UK and Australia (described in part one), we conducted a lot of research amongst smokers to understand what would be most effective at persuading them to quit successfully. We regularly asked why they continued to smoke, when in the vast majority of cases smokers knew (and believed) it was bad for them.[172]

It was extremely rare to find a smoker who denied the overwhelming scientific evidence that smoking increases the risk of established (and

---

172 In Australia, 97% of smokers are aware of at least some of the dangers of smoking (Australian National Preventative Health Agency).

usually fatal) illnesses, such as lung cancer, heart disease and emphysema. Yet, despite conscious knowledge that their habit could kill them, they still smoked.[173]

I described in the introduction how this was where my interest in the irrational, hidden drivers of human behaviour started. What was equally fascinating was how people sought to explain away their reasons for continuing to smoke, and justify it, rather than simply admit it was through a failure of willpower – or because quitting is so hard.

I heard first-hand many different reasons why smokers persisted, for example:

"I always smoke outside so it's only harming me."

"I'll quit when the time is right."

"It's worth the risk."

"I enjoy it. I'm only losing a few of the bad years at the end of my life anyway."

And so on.

Smokers were giving these reasons to make themselves (and others) feel better about their habit. They were post-rationalisations: illogical rationales used to justify their habit, when they consciously knew it was detrimental to their health. These were ways of avoiding cognitive dissonance: the unpleasant sensation when we realise our thoughts and actions are inconsistent.

I don't mean to imply that smokers were consciously deceiving us (lying) – it was pretty clear they really *believed* these reasons. It was their subconscious convincing them that their course of action was the right one, against all rational logic.

Smoking is only one example. There are all sorts of ways in which we construct confabulations, or counter-factuals, to explain our behaviour. In his book, *The Choice Factory*, Richard Shotton describes how the National Survey of Sexual Attitudes and Lifestyles (NATSAL) surveyed 15,000 respondents in 2010, and found that heterosexual women claim to have had a mean of eight sexual partners – whilst heterosexual men claim 12. This logical impossibility is a result of some people (mostly men) over-claiming, and/or some (mostly women) under-claiming in the data.[174]

---

173 Although most smokers have tried to quit at least once. A Canadian study amongst 1,277 smokers from 2016 suggested the average smoker requires 30 attempts at quitting before they are successful (bmjopen.bmj.com/content/6/6/e011045).

174 It's possible that some of the variance may be due to men and women defining sex

Jonathan Haidt, author of *The Righteous Mind,* describes the logical, system-2 mind as thinking of itself as "the Oval Office when actually it's the press office."

It is well established that instinctive, automatic, system-1 processes actually account for a lot of our decision-making – it seems that our slower, reflective, system-2 processes then often seek to take the credit.

Telling stories in research

Post-rationalisation manifests in all sorts of ways in consumer research. I lost count of the number of quantitative, brand tracking research presentations I saw where TV was the most recalled medium used by an advertiser (i.e. the medium on which people most remembered seeing an ad), despite the advertiser not having used TV for years – and in some cases, never.

When conducting qualitative research in a focus group setting, or in one-to-one interviews, a whole host of other biases may also come into play. Duncan Smith is MD of market research agency, MindLab, who specialise in more implicit techniques to uncover these biases.

These types of "approaches to research are really useful when either people don't care about what you're asking, or they post-rationalise to a degree that basically starts to make no sense," says Smith. "So when you're asking people about different packaging variations on a bottle of bleach, nobody really cares. And then you ask people in a group setting, and you listen to somebody who sounds as though they've got a bit of gravitas, they'll go with that opinion, because they didn't really have one in the first place."

It is hard to believe that consumers are deliberately post-rationalising in these circumstances. As Smith says, no one outside the marketing industry cares enough to construct a mental narrative about whether the last ad for butter they saw was on TV or not. When asked, we may vaguely recall seeing an ad, and to reassure ourselves that we have a good memory (if that fits with our self-image) assume that it was on TV – probably because TV has the highest mental availability (explained on page 14). Or be swayed by someone else's more deeply held opinion, especially if they have some authority (see page 68 on authority bias).

---

differently, but, assuming the researchers gave subjects a clear definition, this represents a difference in perception and memory characteristic of post-rationalisation.

Post-rationalisation is a major feature of traditional market research because of the general unreliability of human memory. Most market research asks customers to account for things they have done in the past (claimed behaviour) – rather than ask them at the time (or even before) – and so our remembered reasons will often be inaccurate, and subject to bias as a consequence.

The trouble is, our brains cannot tell the difference between true and false memories. We have all been in arguments with friends and relatives about shared experiences where our recollection of the event differs. When confronted with evidence that proves us incorrect (a photo, for example) it is a very discombobulating, dissonant feeling, which we understandably seek to avoid.

This is not just a problem for market research. Obtaining accurate information on past behaviour is a hugely important challenge for law enforcement, for example. Criminal cases will often hinge on two (or more) people's separate recollections of an event, especially in the absence of observed behaviour (e.g. CCTV footage) or forensic data.[175] Dr Julia Shaw, a psychological and memory scientist at University College London (who has spent over a decade researching police interviewing and emotional memories) describes memories as "stories that we tell ourselves to make sense of our lives."

Given the flaws in our memories for important events like these, simply asking people to account for, or recall, more mundane behaviour – like what we bought in our last supermarket shop – will be deeply flawed as a research methodology.

We are poor prediction machines

Similarly, asking people to forecast future behaviour can be just as prone to bias. We saw in part three that humans, unlike robots, gather small amounts of data to make predictive decisions and then use heuristics and biases to judge the outcome of those choices. In effect, we make best guesses most of the time, because we have neither the time nor capability to collate all

---

175 Part of the reason recent advances in forensic research (especially using DNA) have been such a breakthrough in criminology is because it provides more reliable, objective evidence than witness testimony, which is often hugely unreliable for some of the reasons described here.

available data. If those heuristics and biases are largely subconscious, prone to error, or simply noisy, it follows that it is really hard for us to accurately predict how we might behave in a future scenario.

Consequently, we will often predict that in the future we will behave in a more considered, rational fashion (i.e. more Spock than Homer) than we subsequently do. Anyone who has ever set themselves a monthly household budget will recognise this phenomenon. In behavioural science, this is explained by concepts like the intention-action gap, optimism bias and the planning fallacy (see below).

Any business that relies purely on predictions of consumers' future behaviour to make decisions therefore runs a very significant risk – each consumer you ask is making a (biased) guess. Multiply that by the hundreds or thousands in your sample and the predicted outcomes are essentially random. This explains why thousands of product launches fail every year, despite market research identifying that sufficient numbers of people intend to buy the product to make it successful.

For example, when the Trinity Mirror launched *New Day* in 2016, an extensively researched, positive, politically neutral newspaper – it lasted less than three months before closing.

"At the end of the day, what consumers told us they would do, and what they actually did, were different things," said Trinity Mirror CEO Simon Fox.[176]

New products that fail in research often succeed in the real world for the same reason. In part two we saw that econometric modelling based on consumer data incorrectly forecast that Amazon Prime would be a failure. Likewise, Red Bull is supposedly one of the worst market researched products ever. Consumers thought it tasted disgusting. As Rory Sutherland points out, why would anyone say buying a foul-tasting fizzy drink, that comes in a smaller can than Coke and costs three times as much, was a good idea?

As of 2017, Red Bull has the highest market share of any energy drink in the world, with 6.3bn cans sold in a year.

---

176 www.cityam.com/trinity-mirror-boss-new-day-newspaper-failed-because/

OPTIMISM BIAS AND THE PLANNING FALLACY

At the time of writing,[177] it has just been announced that the HS2 rail project – a high-speed rail link between London and the West Midlands – planned to open at the end of 2026, may not actually be completed until five years later. The cost has also grown from £62bn to between £81bn and £88bn.[178]

London's new east to west railway service, Crossrail, was originally estimated to cost £15.4 billion and open in December 2018. However, in 2018 it was announced that the project would require a further £1.4 billion and open in late 2020 or early 2021.[179]

This is not just a failure of British infrastructure planning. In Berlin, construction on a new airport (Berlin Brandenberg) started in 2006 after almost 15 years of planning, with the opening originally scheduled for 2011. It is still yet to open – the most realistic estimate is now 2021.[180]

Major projects like this – with billions invested and the finest engineering minds on the planet working on them – regularly exceed timing and spending estimates. Kahneman and Tversky first suggested this is routinely due to the planning fallacy – that our predictions about time needed to complete future tasks are subject to an optimism bias, and we regularly underestimate the time needed. On huge projects like these the combined effect of multiple individuals being biased in this way can lead to large effects, and massive underestimates of cost and resources.

Our optimism bias means we believe that we are less likely to experience a negative event than others. In this part of the book we have seen a prime example: smokers regularly believed they were less likely to experience a smoking-related illness than others, and that they would find it easier to quit. This would then be used as a justification to delay quitting.

The result is that, when we are planning, we neglect potential setbacks and their likelihoods. It is why we always have less money

---

177 September 2019.
178 www.bbc.co.uk/news/business-49563549
179 www.bbc.co.uk/news/uk-england-london-48054789
180 www.bbc.co.uk/news/world-48527308

in the bank at the end of the month than we expect, and is one reason predictions of our future behaviour are frequently inaccurate.

This is not just important to remember for engineering businesses – any project is likely to be subject to this bias. In many businesses, timing estimates have a standard contingency added to counter this effect.

And, yet again, it demonstrates that humans are not perfect, robot-like, prediction machines.

The role for traditional market research

Does the human tendency to post-rationalise, and our poor predictive ability, mean all traditional market research is useless?

Leigh Caldwell is co-founder of The Irrational Agency, and specialises in using more implicit research techniques to uncover the nonconscious drivers of decision-making.

"The value of [traditional research methods] is that they are cheap and easy. But consumer's predictions of their own purchase likelihoods correlate about 50% of the time with their own purchasing behaviour," Caldwell says. "So if your competitors have got 70% accuracy because they have a better method then you are not going to do very well. If you are making a €5bn investment in launching a new car brand is it worth saving €10,000 in cheaper, less accurate market research methods that put you at a disadvantage? It's clearly worth investing a bit more in methods that give you a 70–80% chance of predicting the truth."

Fifty percent accuracy is still much better than none, so if a business wants to understand the more conscious, system-2 drivers of decision-making, then traditional techniques will give useful data. Additionally, adopting sophisticated questioning and research techniques, getting as close in time as possible to the behaviour itself, and replicating the context of decision-making, can minimise some of the biases and inaccuracies involved in asking about claimed behaviour.

Asking better questions will give you better answers – so engaging researchers familiar with behavioural biases is critical.

Duncan Smith described to me how there is actually value in the contradictions this sometimes throws up – because it illustrates the importance of context. "We found it difficult at MindLab over the years to try and get people to change their outlook on research," he says. "Because essentially, what we're telling people (in nice enough ways) is what you've been doing has been wrong. It's not a great starting point for a discussion. I think the idea of using an understanding of these implicit or gut measures is to complement what people say. And when they both agree, then you've got some good solid research. When you find that there's a contradiction between what people say and what they do, what we find implicitly and what we find explicitly, that sometimes scares people, because they're thinking that there's something wrong with the model. But what it actually is, is explaining context."

Richard Shotton concludes that different (often multiple) approaches are required. "All methodologies are flawed, the key is to know what the flaw is. Use a mixed approach," he advocates.

Using evidence, not intuitions, is a critical test-tube behaviour – any business that wishes to avoid the dangers of post-rationalisation and poor prediction in market research should simply *stop just asking people to account for their actions*. Or at least stop this being the only source of insight, or the default.

Instead, where possible supplement with data on actual, observed behaviour (we saw in part two that this characterises the most successful 21st-century businesses), and use predictive methods that look at the more implicit, subconscious influences. There are huge competitive advantages to using other techniques to understand what is really influencing your customers – rather than just believing what they tell you.

In the rest of this part, we will see how using more sophisticated research tools and techniques enable businesses to better understand the more hidden system-1 influences on customer decision-making.

CHAPTER 18

The Importance of Subconscious Associations – Understanding How People Buy, at Home and in Business

Why are subconscious associations important?

A T THIS POINT, you might be pondering something like this: if much of our behaviour is driven by unconscious influences which are not revealed by speaking to people, why bother researching amongst your customers at all? Does adopting test-tube behaviours not just involve running continuous experiments to determine what works in real world environments?

It is a very good question, and, as we have seen, companies like Google and Amazon do exactly this. But those businesses have some innate advantages: billions of robust data points on actual behaviour, and products that are relatively simple and homogenous. Ultimately, everyone's experience of using Google and Amazon is basically the same – a search query, followed by a series of results,[181] which may or may not prompt a click or purchase.

---

181 This is, of course, only true of Google's core search engine product. Google's parent, Alphabet, has diversified into a wide range of products and services, including Google Docs, Maps, Assistant, and so on.

A fast-moving consumer goods (FMCG) brand like a shampoo, for example, does not have this luxury. Their products are available for sale via multiple physical retailers, websites and environments. It may have many product variants, features and ranges. Likewise, a business-to-business (B2B) product like invoicing software may sell to multiple categories, via multiple vendors, intermediaries and channels.

These brands will have many variables that influence the purchase decision, both conscious and nonconscious, and the context for each decision will be different. Are they buying the shampoo for themselves, or a family member? Is their business a small sole-trader – or are they buying software for thousands of employees? Discretely controlling for these when testing or observing can be very hard.

In these circumstances conducting tests in real-world environments becomes complicated, and expensive, given the wide ranges of channels and variables involved. Having some understanding of what is actually driving the decision to purchase before you decide about new product development, service design, and other important investments (even if the decision is simply what to test), is therefore a necessity – otherwise, you are simply relying on guess work.

As with AI and machine learning tools – if you want to create a better prediction machine, you need better training data. We saw in the last chapter that the data you get from directly asking your customers will largely only account for the conscious, system-2 drivers of behaviour. It is now well-established that most purchase decisions are actually driven by a number of subconscious associations. How do businesses find out what is really going on in our customers heads to help make predictions, and remove the risk in betting on launching new products and services?

How subconscious associations influence how we buy

Fortunately, we are now much better at finding insights into subconscious drivers of decision-making because of advances in both behavioural science and technology. As a result, we can gain useful insights on how to influence behaviour.

In the next chapter, we shall see some examples of these new technologies and approaches. They demonstrate that by re-creating the real-life context of decision-making, and replicating the mental processes that your customers go through when making those purchase decisions, they can illustrate the hidden influences not revealed by simply asking them why.

First, it is worth considering how the findings of behavioural science inform how we think about customers. In particular, how and why people generally choose to buy certain products and services – and not others.

A quick thought experiment to illustrate the point. Have you ever been in a foreign country, where you do not speak the language (or at least not well), and had to visit a supermarket to make a purchase?[182] It's hard, isn't it? When robbed of one of the key inputs into our decision-making – recognisable brands and product descriptions – it is almost impossible to know what the hell anything is, and therefore choose the right product for our needs. In the days before Google Translate, you might end up shaking packets, peering inside or smelling things to make sure you were buying sugar, not salt (or vice versa).

When I spoke with Eaon Pritchard, author of *Where Did It All Go Wrong: Adventures at the Dunning-Kruger Peak of Advertising*, we shared our stories of first moving to Australia (Eaon originally hails from Aberdeen). Even with a (mostly) shared language, buying the right products was hopelessly difficult, and largely a matter of trial and error – or relying on social proof.[183]

"My wife sent me out to buy washing powder," says Pritchard. "I went to the supermarket and I was just paralysed. I didn't know what to do. All these brands I'd never heard of. I thought 'I'll just wait here and see what someone else is buying, and buy that.'"

In our hometown, walk into a supermarket and you are instantly confronted with a wealth of information and semiotic signals to guide your decision-making. This will be everything from recognisable brand names, product aisle descriptions, even simple colours (to signify the supermarket's own brand, for example). If these capture our attention, and trigger the right associations, we are more likely to make a purchase.

Many of these associations are subconscious, and so understanding these will allow your business to influence or change them. Those that are easier to bring to mind, that is more mentally available,[184] will be more influential – particularly for more instinctive, system-1 decisions.

---

182 Thanks to Tom Roach from BBH, whose tweet on this prompted the experiment.
183 Explained on page 10.
184 See page 14.

In the next part, we will see that behavioural and marketing science have identified that building more mentally available brand associations is the primary purpose of marketing. But it is not the only way to build these associations. Understanding the mental architecture (or prioritisation of different decision-making criteria) that influence the decision to purchase is important – as it will determine where to focus your efforts.

We are predictably irrational at work as well as at home

That applies to well-known, recognisable brands, like Coca-Cola or Apple, you might think. Those brands have spent billions over many years building strong subconscious associations with their products.

If your business operates in the B2B world, or has a new, less well-known, or niche product, you might think that there won't be any relevant associations with that brand. Or that the decision to purchase is primarily governed by utilitarian, system-2 factors, like relative price (how expensive is it compared to other similar products) or perceived value (what I get for that price), or key product features. Surely here the decision to purchase is more Spock than Homer?

If you work in a business that requires you to market to other businesses, then you might also think that marketing works in a more rational, linear fashion, because your customers are more rational. That a business decision-maker is deciding on behalf of a business, and it is not their money, so surely they are deciding based on more objective, system-2 criteria?

Once again, the evidence suggests otherwise. Most purchase decisions are still made by humans, after all. Research by CEB Global (now Gartner) and Google, amongst 3,000 B2B decision-makers across 36 brands and 7 categories, found that personal value (i.e. the professional, social, emotional and self-image benefits) was twice as important as business value (i.e. the functional benefits and business outcomes).

"Not only do emotions matter in B2B buying, but they actually matter even more than logic and reason. This finding highlights a potentially untapped opportunity for marketers to reposition brands around personal value," the research concluded.[185]

---

185 www.cebglobal.com/content/dam/cebglobal/us/EN/best-practices-decision-support/

Duncan Smith agrees. "If we are working in an industry that's perceived as more rational, such as B2B instead of B2C," he says. "Then there is almost an understanding that the people stop behaving as human beings just because they're making decisions at work and not at home, which is completely ludicrous. And the same in pharmaceuticals, or with doctors. A number of times we've seen very expensive research conducted because people want to ask an oncologist about whether the colour blue stands out more than yellow. But it is not an oncologist question. It is a human question."

Homer in the city

One business that understands this well is Turtl, a start-up that applies insights from behavioural science and psychology to create better business publications. In effect, they take the often long, boring, and frequently unread paper documents that businesses create, and turn them into online documents that are more likely to be engaged with and ultimately acted upon. Their platform captures data on who is reading what, and what chapters and topics readers care about, and their clients include businesses like Cisco, Allianz and The Economist. Their company mission is to 'kill the PDF'.

"What we do is encourage people to think differently about reading and about the reader," says Nick Mason, Turtl's founder. "And not everyone wants to read everything. And not everyone wants to read everything in the same order as everyone else. By providing people with more options around what to read, and when to read it and allowing them to explore, that's what speaks to the intrinsic motivation side of things.

"And what we find with a lot of customers is that they get feedback from people saying: 'I love the format, I really enjoyed reading it'. There's a tendency in B2B historically that people think when you put on a suit, it's all serious, and suddenly you stop being human and you become a machine. But the thing that we play to is the fact that that's not only not true, but you're actually more likely to be emotionally influenced than not. We just try and help people use these techniques like visuals, animation

---

marketing-communications/pdfs/promotion-emotion-whitepaper-full.pdf 'From Promotion to Emotion: Connecting B2B Customers to Brands', CEB Marketing Leadership Council in partnership with Google (2013).

and transitions, using the layout so that you end up with something that is a good few steps above what they've seen for the rest of their working day."

Even when the decisions involve large sums of money, such as in financial markets, people are just as irrational, prone to post-rationalisation, and emotional. Homer works in the city, as well as at the nuclear power plant.

Hannah Lewis, founder of Mindmafia.com and Behave London, described a project to me on the barriers to financial trustees in major financial institutions adopting environmental, social and governance practices, otherwise known as responsible investing (or ESG). By digging deeper, and going beyond what people were simply saying, she found a richer, more truthful, source of insights.

"The justifications they were giving for not investing responsibly were wholly fiscal," Lewis says. "There isn't the proof, it's a fad, and so on. We tested on that basis, giving them information versus no information. And what we found out was that 25% of trustees simply did not know what the acronym stood for, despite the ESG acronym being used as standard throughout the industry. The barrier was actually that they were unwilling to admit their lack of knowledge."

In a business context, we are as emotional, irrational, and Homer-like as we are elsewhere in our lives – if not more so. We saw in the previous part the impact this has on our behaviours in the workplace. When making purchase decisions for our business, the heuristics and biases seem to compel us to behave in ways that ensure we minimise risk (i.e. be loss averse) – both reputationally and financially.

Business decision-making involves considerable personal and professional risk, so to some extent it makes sense that we seek to minimise the chances of disaster. If I buy the wrong brand of shampoo, the consequences are pretty inconsequential. If I make a bad business decision, I could lose my job, my income and my house. When the stakes are that high, it is no wonder that the decision becomes an emotional, not a rational, one.

IBM famously had a long-running advertising slogan that cleverly captured this tendency towards loss aversion amongst business purchasers: "No one ever got fired for buying IBM."

One might cheekily update it to how most decisions are also made about consumer research: "No one ever got fired for asking people what they think."

Focus on satisficers, not maximisers

In business or elsewhere, whenever there are multiple options to choose from (typically more than six, due to the capacity of our short-term memory), as there are in most purchase decisions, the paradox of choice comes into effect.[186] In the foreign supermarket, the problem is we have no way to narrow down the several thousand options, which makes choosing impossible – because the risks of disaster (buying sugar instead of salt, for example) are high. Even when we do have the knowledge and associations to narrow our choices, for most decisions we are simply looking for something to quickly and easily meet choice-satisficing criteria, which may often be subconscious.

"If someone went to the shampoo aisle and spent an hour analyzing the price, the expected utility and so on," says Richard Shotton, "you would think that person was insane. It's essentially sensible to buy the most popular one, the one that's been on TV, the one that springs to your mind. Because if you buy the most popular brand it might not be the most objectively perfect, but it's very unlikely to be crap.

"A lot of behavioural science and social psychology shows that much of our decision-making is not about maximising potential gain. It's about minimising risk."

One other conclusion about customers is that products and services that simplify difficult choices can generate much more loyalty, as we saw with the FANGs in part two. For example, one development since Schwartz wrote *The Paradox of Choice* has been the explosion of internet aggregator sites such as comparethemarket, uSwitch and GoCompare. They allow us to choice-satisfice decisions in low-interest (i.e. functional) categories like banking, insurance, utilities, and travel, using more objective, system-2 criteria like price, and product features and benefits.

The growth of this market in the UK has been astonishing – from a non-existent base 15 years ago, Moneysupermarket is now valued at over £1bn.[187] Beyond the ads themselves, people seem to have an enormous favourability to these brands, seeing them as consumer champions, and simplifying the complexities of modern life.[188] It is hard to imagine many

---

186   See page 50.
187   www.telegraph.co.uk/finance/personalfinance/10894742/Are-price-comparison-websites-too-powerful.html
188   Even though the article ibid. suggests that in some cases they may be colluding with the

financial service companies being able to inspire such endearment towards cuddly Russian meerkats.

Once a purchase is made, for low-interest and low-knowledge decisions like this most people are usually happy enough to stick with their existing product or service, if it does the job reasonably well. On average people in the UK spend longer in a relationship with their bank than with their husband or wife, for example.[189] Our inertia bias (driven by loss aversion and ingrained habits) makes switching a difficult behaviour to change, and is another reason why so many new products fail.

By contrast, the more expertise and interest someone has in a category, the more likely they are to maximise and want more choices, rather than less. In the famous jam experiment, the effect was reversed amongst jam experts – because they preferred as much choice as possible. Maximisers are more likely to shop around (as they actively seek the best possible choice), but paradoxically this means they are of less long-term value – because as soon as someone produces a better product or service, they will likely switch again.[190]

The problem is the person who chooses the range of products or services a business sells will likely be an expert in that category – and may assume most consumers want that same variety of choice.

For example, in my local consumer electronics store the shelves are stocked with every possible variant of toaster – different colours, brands, sizes and prices, over 20 models – because the retail buyer has the specialist knowledge to tell the relative difference between them, and assumes it increases the chances of a consumer finding one they like.

But I, like most customers, am not a toaster expert. I am simply looking for a toaster that meets a simple shortlist of criteria: that it will reliably toast bread without burning the house down. Buying a toaster in this context is a hopelessly hard problem, and I am likely to leave the store, go online and simply buy the Amazon best-seller instead. As in most categories, there will be many more toaster satisficers than maximisers.

Businesses should consequently focus on researching on how to influence purchase decisions by satisficers rather than maximisers. These people may only regard your brand as good enough – because it is cognitively easy to

---

products themselves, and most are not independently owned.
189   www.theguardian.com/money/2013/sep/07/switching-banks-seven-day
190   We shall see an example of this in the savings "rate tarts", described in chapter 22.

buy, rather than objectively better than the competition – but they are both more numerous, and if you are successful, more loyal.

And, both of these factors make them more profitable, in the long term.[191]

Helping customers make easy, good enough decisions

When a customer makes a choice about what to purchase, there will be nonconscious influences at play driven by the context of that decision. There is no such thing as a neutral choice architecture. The simple fact of making a decision triggers a host of system-1 biases and heuristics we are not consciously aware of.

Being in the behaviour business means understanding that customers purchase decision-making depends on the nonconscious (and conscious) associations of your product or service. If it is the cognitively easiest to buy, and minimises the perceived risks of a bad choice – whether that be a choice-satisficing or -maximising decision – it is more likely to be bought. And what we now know is that, in most circumstances, customers are very happy to be satificers and go for good enough, because, for most of us, there are very few circumstances in which we are willing to invest the time to make the best possible decision.

The abundance of choice now available for every purchase decision means it is simply not worth the effort.

What most consumers actually crave is choices made simpler. For example, a former client (a leading national newspaper) used to offer over 120 different subscription options via their website. When we reduced this down to eight, they increased sales by nearly 5%.

Choice maximising requires cognitive effort and, as lazy cognitive misers, we seek to avoid this wherever possible. Ultimately, those products which have the highest mental availability that meet our key criteria – whether it be rational or emotional – are much more likely to be bought.

Eaon Pritchard succinctly summarises these insights into purchasing from behavioural science – and the implications for marketing – in his book, *Where Did It All Go Wrong*:

---

191 We will examine this more in the next part, in relation to light users.

"The consumers we have to communicate with spend precious little time thinking about brands, do next to no evaluation around most purchase decisions, and even brands they use and like are trivial in comparison to the rest of their daily lives.

"Rather than engagement, conversations or participation people's actual buying behaviour is about reducing complexity, reducing choice and making easier, good-enough decisions.

"Our job is simply about getting brands noticed, remembered at the appropriate time and then bought."

The implication of these insights into purchase decision-making is we need new ways to understand what gets brands and products noticed and remembered, and the mental architecture (i.e. criteria) that surrounds those decisions – the subject of the next chapter.

CHAPTER 19

Gaining Advantageous Insights – Techniques and Tools to Better Understand Customers

Recreating context

I N THIS PART, we have seen that finding insights into what your customers' nonconscious, system-1 criteria are for decision-making requires more sophisticated techniques than simply asking them to account for, or predict, their behaviour. One way of doing this is to focus on actual, rather than claimed, behaviour – either by looking at past data, or replicating the context as closely as possible and running live experiments (employing test-tube behaviours).

Throughout this book, we have also seen multiple examples of the importance of context in decision-making. The fundamental attribution error (see overleaf), perhaps the most important contribution of social psychology to behavioural science, is evidence that we frequently underestimate the importance of context. Even when using more traditional research techniques, accurately recreating the context of a decision will give you a better understanding of influences on the behaviour.

In the case of purchase decisions, this could mean literally recreating the physical environment. PRS IN VIVO is a shopper research agency that has created ShopperLabs around the world – real-life replicas of actual stores complete with aisles, tills and signage – as well as performed shopper studies in store.

The advantage of these lab studies over field studies is that it is much easier to change the variables in the test environment (shelf configurations, alternate branding and so on), making it easy to implement test-tube behaviours, and test and learn.

Combining more sophisticated research techniques with accurate recreations of the real-world context can be hugely insightful. In these ShopperLabs, PRS IN VIVO will often employ eye-tracking glasses[192] to see what people are looking at, and where their attention is drawn. Participants will be given tasks or missions to complete (such as a shopping list) to reflect a real-life context, rather than simply allowing them to wander aimlessly.[193]

Eric Singler is director general of the BVA Group (parent company of PRS IN VIVO) as well as founder of the BVA Nudge Unit, and has been implementing these studies around the world for over 25 years.

He says that the realism of the laboratory setting is critical: "The greater this realism, the more the limitations rightly highlighted by the advocates of field experiments seem to fade away. If the laboratory setting closely mirrors that of real life, it follows that the results obtained should be able to predict real life results ... On the other hand, if the laboratory conditions are poorly matched to the natural environment in which the decision takes place (it's not only a question of the physical environment but also the setting's ability to recreate the right mindset in the participants) then the results may not be reproduced."[194]

Whether your business's brand is stocked in a supermarket or not, conducting these kind of real-world, contextually-accurate tests need not require huge sample sizes, nor massive budgets.

---

192   These are glasses with tiny cameras built in, which allow researchers to see where people's gaze is at any given moment. Researchers can therefore see what subjects are looking at, and where, and for how long. As much of the information absorbed may be processed subconsciously, it can be extremely useful for assessing salience (explained on page 14). The disadvantage of this method is that participants are more aware that they are participating in research, which can trigger the Hawthorne Effect (the phenomenon where social science experiment outcomes are affected simply by participants knowing that they are part of an experiment).

193   My colleague Ted Utoft, a senior qualitative director at PRS IN VIVO, tells me that research subjects often go into system-1 mode in the lab and start completing their weekly shop, arriving at the checkout with a full basket or trolley that they then expect to pay for and take home!

194   *Nudge Marketing*, Singler E, Pearson (2015).

"There's a hell of a lot that can be done with very simple field experiments where you do four things," says Richard Shotton. "One: you create a situation as similar to the purchase situation as possible. Two: ensure people don't know they are being tested, so they behave naturally. Three: you keep every variable the same, apart from one – the thing you are testing. Four: you want to have a reasonably representative sample, because representativeness is more important than the size of the sample … If you don't need absolute certainty, and the effect you are looking for is reasonably large, you will pick it up on a sample of a couple of hundred. A lot of the classic experiments in psychology were done with a sample of 50 or 60."

FUNDAMENTAL ATTRIBUTION ERROR

A thought experiment: imagine you are interviewing someone for a job at 2pm. The allotted time arrives, and there is no sign of the interviewee. The clock ticks on, still no sign. Finally, they arrive at 2:27, somewhat flustered and bedraggled.

"I'm so sorry," they say. "My train got stuck in a tunnel for an hour so I had no phone signal, and couldn't let you know I was running late. And when I got to the station there were no taxis, so I had to call for one. By the time I could use my phone I was nearly here."

Would you give them the job?

I have given you no information about their skills, competencies or experience to do the role. But it is not a great first impression, right? Who is to say this kind of thing doesn't happen all the time, and they are one of those people who are always late? Or just have perennial bad luck? What if this had been an important meeting or presentation?

But look back at the circumstances of their lateness. None of the things that happened were their fault. You could say that they should have planned better and left earlier – but if the train had been on time they would have been half an hour early. To think that any of these factors affects their ability to do the job is wholly irrational.

This is an example of the fundamental attribution error: the phenomenon by which people tend to attribute behaviour to innate personality traits or character, when they are often more likely due to external factors. Put simply: we tend to think what people do reflects who they are. In this case, we perceive that their lateness shows a lack of consideration or concern for us, or interest in the job full stop.[195]

In a classic experiment, Jones and Harris (1967) had Duke University students read debaters' speeches supporting or attacking Cuba's leader, Fidel Castro. When told that the debater chose which position to take, students logically enough assumed it reflected the person's own attitude.

But what happened when the students were told that the debate coach instructed them whether to be pro- or anti-Castro? Even knowing this, students still believed that the debater believed what they were saying. People seemed to think, "Yeah, I know they were told to say that, but, you know, I still think they really believe it."[196]

I find the fundamental attribution error to be hugely useful and instructive when thinking about the behaviour of colleagues, clients, customers and people in general. It is hugely helpful in developing empathy. If a high-performing colleague's performance, enthusiasm and interest in their work suddenly declines, it is unlikely to be because they have become bad at their job overnight.

We shall see throughout this book that one of the key findings of behavioural science is that context is hugely relevant to shaping behaviour – fundamental attribution error explains why we often fail to see it.

Knowing if you will be noticed

In the same way, assessing the impact of marketing in changing behaviour (i.e. ensuring a product is noticed, remembered and bought) is much more effective if the context in which the message is received by (potential) customers is recreated. Mike Follett is the MD and co-founder of Lumen Research, who also use eye-tracking technology to evaluate marketing

---

195   In this particular case, the representative heuristic (explained on page 16) also means that we have taken one example to reflect a general trend, and then equated that to some flaw in the character of the interviewee.

196   Jones, E. E.; Harris, V. A., (1967). 'The attribution of attitudes', *Journal of Experimental Social Psychology*, 3 (1): 1–24.

effectiveness, or as he puts it: "To work out what people are looking at, and also what they are ignoring."

They use the technology to see how people actually respond when consuming advertisements in context – unlike the traditional, non-realistic testing approaches of a focus group (e.g. in a room eating pizza with strangers), or a quantitative survey (e.g. filling out a questionnaire at the kitchen table). In their research, participants view stimulus via their own computer or mobile phone, using the in-built webcam to see what they are looking at – meaning there is no need to employ glasses technology.[197] This allows for large, representative sample sizes to be used.

To assess digital advertising, research participants simply allow access via their webcam and start browsing as normal. They are then shown ads in a relevant context, and their responses are anonymously recorded. Other types of advertising can be tested by placing TV ads amongst normal programming, or using realistic videos of a typical journey when out of home (such as walking down a street, with the relevant ad digitally inserted). The context of this exposure to marketing is more realistic, both because respondents are at home and relaxed, and they are seeing the ad in the context of other ads and content without external influences (unlike in a focus group). Based on this work, Lumen have gathered huge amounts of data to create benchmarks by industry and channel.

This data shows that driving attention – more than engagement – is critical to marketing effectiveness. It may seem obvious but is often forgotten. By some estimates, the average adult is exposed to over 3,000 different messages every day – the vast majority are simply ignored. It follows if people don't notice an ad then it won't change their behaviour, so whether it stands out in context (i.e. is salient) is critical.

"Things that are not threatening, aren't interesting, and aren't useful are easy to ignore," says Follett. "People are not better at ignoring stuff, there is just more stuff for people to ignore ... We use eye-tracking to predict likely levels of attention. It turns out in general, people are more likely to look at ads they can see, than ads they can't see, and ads that are in view for a long time are more likely to be seen than those that are not. Using this data we can make predictions about the past – and the future."

---

197   The tech uses facial recognition to identify where their gaze is drawn on the screen. This tech has to be authorised by the participants to do this, and is automatically deleted once the research is complete, so the participants privacy is not compromised.

For their client, British Gas, they found this model of "predictive attention" was a key driver of the effectiveness of online advertising – attention predicted not just clicks, but sales. This was then built into the digital media buying strategy, allowing British Gas to focus spend on online ads that drove attention (i.e. were effective), rather than delivered the most impressions (i.e. number of people exposed, a measure of cost-efficiency).

"The bad news is that we have pushed up their CPMs [cost per impression] by 54%," says Follett. "We've ended up making them buy more expensive media. But the good news is that sales have gone up by 239%. The profit ROI they have made on this is between 10 and 13 times. So this attention stuff works."

Subconscious associations – knowing what people really think

These approaches allow businesses to test the impact of changes in the context of decision-making, such as where products sit on the shelf or where they are advertised, to focus on more effectively garnering attention. But once you have your customers attention, how do you find out what they are *really* thinking? How do you know exactly what the hidden, nonconscious, emotional drivers of their decision to purchase (or not) are? To do this, methods that look at implicit motivations are needed.

This does not require literally getting inside your customers heads. There are research methods available based on neuroscience that seek to correlate what happens in our brain with our behaviour – but, ultimately, the evidence on these is disputed and the techniques are expensive.

And when you can assess the outcome in terms of actual behaviour, why go to the middle-man?

"There are easy ways to try and understand what's going on in people's minds without having to wire people's brains up," says Duncan Smith. "And to be honest, the use of medical equipment like EEG[198] is not particularly useful in giving you much insight. It'll tell you how hard people are thinking, whether and when they're paying attention, whether their

---

198 An electroencephalograph (EEG) is a medical device where electrical activity in the brain is measured by attaching electrodes to the scalp, and tracking and recording brain waves. Needless to say, the inventors of the tech probably didn't anticipate it would be used to find out what brand of crisps people prefer.

heads are 'in' or heads are 'out', but it doesn't give us much else. We're using psychology-based tools in the lab as well, which is generally known as implicit testing, and using them to try and better understand how people make decisions."

An Implicit Association Test (IAT) is a methodology that identifies automatic associations by giving people word- or image-based sorting tasks, then records speed of response as well as the response itself. The theory is that faster responses indicate a more implicit (or subconscious, system-1) decision.

The most famous is the Harvard IAT,[199] which evaluates whether participants have unconscious biases based on race, gender, or age. People are required to sort positive or negative words based on whether they associate them with pictures of black or white faces (for example). This test is controversial,[200] but for less contentious issues the approach can give useful insights into instinctive decision-making.

"If a piece of research is truly implicit we're not asking people to make any decisions at all, we're just looking at how they behave when they make certain decisions," says Smith. "Pure implicit association testing is really useful because you can't really cheat it, because we're looking at people making decisions in about one second. Most implicit testing is all based around speed of response …We don't wire people's brains up anymore. We're just looking at measuring people's intuitive responses, because this instinctual response actually drives more of our behaviour than we think."

Like all the methods described in this chapter, IATs are relatively inexpensive, and so are not beyond the reach of small businesses with limited budgets. Digital platforms allow implicit research to be conducted quickly and at scale – when I was at Ogilvy, we created an implicit platform for mobile devices using functionality popularised by Tinder. Participants simply sorted words or images by either swiping left or right. We used this in a project for a council to see whether people instinctively knew which items to put in which recycling bin – see a picture of a milk carton, and swipe left for plastic, right for paper. The speed or response indicated whether this was known instinctively or not – after all, recycling is not the

---

199   Available to complete for free online at implicit.harvard.edu/implicit

200   The controversy relates to the replicability of the methodology (there is evidence that the same respondents get different results at different times), as well as the nature of unconscious bias itself. For example, the Harvard IAT is often used to demonstrate to people and organisations that they have problems with diversity, often as part of training programs, but, as we saw in the previous part, there is little evidence that simply telling people that they may be ageist, sexist or racist will change behaviour on its own. The bias is unconscious after all.

kind of decision or behaviour most people spend a lot of time consciously thinking about.

As well as these sophisticated, implicit, technology-driven techniques, there are other simple, fast, and inexpensive ways to get to nonconscious drivers of behaviour.[201]

Jason Smith, whom we met earlier, was previously co-founder and CEO of Blurrt (a social media data agency) and explained to me how they used insights to understand emotional reactions, known as sentiment analysis.

"We had a product that collected social media posts in real time. And then we would analyse the sentiment and emotion, and then that would give insight in a dashboard," he says. "One brand had their whole marketing approach focused on TV advertising. They had changed creative direction, and one ad had what they felt was a message that was slightly close to the mark [controversial]. They were saying it takes 10 days or so for us to get feedback in traditional ways as to whether or not this ad has worked. And because we're a little bit nervous about it we'd like something in real time. Their CEO could log in to our dashboard and could get real time feedback from social media, and a flavour of what people are saying about it, and how they felt about it ...

"They put that into screens within their offices, so that at any point in time you could see the emotional reaction to the brand. They then used those insights in the creative process of making the ads themselves, which then informed what they measured. It was ground-breaking, I think, from a brand perspective and gave some really interesting insights, not only in terms of measuring the campaign, but also shaping the ads that they produced."

---

201 Leigh Caldwell has a theory that there is a system 3 involved in our purchase decisions, that is only revealed by these methods. He describes system 3 as representing the human imagination, and our forecasting about how we will feel about our purchase in the future. "You can use system 2 in making forecasts and predictions," he says. "But it doesn't tell us the value of those forecasts, and it doesn't give us the utility function. And neither can system 1, because that is purely instinctive. System 3 is quite a powerful tool for market research, because what consumers are doing when they are, let's say, thinking about a car, is using their imagination to create the experience of driving that car in advance and to simulate the experience. What we would want to know as market researchers and as a car manufacturer is: how do they do that? How do they construct this car in their heads? And therefore, how do we make their imaginary car as appealing as possible, so that they will buy the real car? How do I communicate with them to support that imaginative process? What does their existing mental model of the world look like? The market research process there is about mapping out the customers imagination as it stands, and then testing out different versions of how I talk about the car and the stories I tell about it."

Preventing post-rationalisation and improving predictions: observing behaviour

The most effective way to predict future behaviour (and therefore business success) is to look at past behaviour. We saw in part two how the leading digital businesses are conducting thousands of experiments every day to gain insights into actual user behaviour. Amazon has billions of data points on what its customers are buying. Google knows what every user is searching for, so it has no need to go out and ask them. Netflix knows what you watch, and Facebook knows what content you engage with. For companies of their size, the FANGs spend a negligible amount on traditional market research.

That is all well and good for these digital behemoths, you might think, but what about non-digital businesses, or those without resources and data on the same scale? The good news is that gaining data on observed behaviour amongst your target audiences is not as hard – or as expensive – as you might expect. The techniques described in this chapter are valuable pre-testing tools available to any business seeking to embed test-tube behaviours, and understand how to influence customers – and they do not break the bank. There is also much you can learn from simply watching how your customers behave.

Returning to our work at the Department of Health on anti-smoking, having realised the flaws in the traditional approach, we looked at the data more deeply and started to observe (rather than ask about) behaviour.

Data showed that smoking prevalence was higher in lower socio-economic groups. Looking at specific occupations, we discovered smoking rates were highest amongst 'routine and manual' occupations.[202] These are typically shift-based, fixed-hour jobs, like factory or shop work – similar to the kind of jobs James Bloodworth experienced in part four.[203]

---

202 Interestingly, this was a much stronger correlation than income alone. Some routine and manual occupations are relatively well-paid e.g. factory supervisors/shop stewards/store managers. Plus, by definition they are in work (and not unemployed). As a result of an ever-increasing taxation policy, smoking is now a very expensive habit – the cost remains one of the most common reasons given for quitting.
203 You may recall that Bloodworth described how working in the Amazon FC (warehouse) had contributed to him taking up smoking again.

To understand why, we conducted an extensive ethnographic study: a technique from anthropological research. Teams of researchers went and spent time with routine and manual smokers, observing them at home, work and play, as well as asking the smokers to fill out diaries recording when and where they smoked during the day.

We found that the nature of 'routine and manual' smokers lives balancing work and family meant that their daily lives were frequently busy and chaotic. Smoking often represented a brief respite, and a ciggie break was seen as welcome relief. The break-based nature of routine and manual work also reinforced the habit loop,[204] and made it harder for them to quit than other smokers.[205]

The research identified the most motivating smoking-related harm that was (critically) impossible for routine and manual smokers to post-rationalise: the impact it had on their family. Smokers who said that they were only harming themselves by smoking, and it was their choice to do so, couldn't rationally explain away that their smoking meant their kids were also much more likely to, nor the proven risks of exposing their loved ones to secondhand (passive) smoke.

These invaluable insights into actual observed smoking behaviour informed campaign development. Working with Kate Waters (whom we met in part one), they informed our new Tobacco Marketing Strategy based on the key motivations and barriers to quitting for routine and manual smokers.

The strategy was to communicate the dangers of smoking to families as a whole (rather than the smokers themselves), and switching emphasis to focus on the support tools available to help routine and manual smokers quit more successfully (described in chapter 2).[206] As a result, the campaign helped deliver the government's Public Service Agreement (PSA) target of reducing smoking rates to 21% or less in 2009 – a year early.

---

204 Explained on page 127.

205 Bloodworth described his experience of smoking whilst working for Amazon as being "… like an emotional palliative in the same way you might put a sticking plaster on your feet after walking ten miles." Ten miles being the average distance he walked each day when working in the FC (warehouse).

206 This included an extensive partnership strategy targeting the major routine and manual employers. It was an easy sell as there was significant benefit to them from getting involved in campaigns to help their staff quit smoking – specifically gaining healthier (and therefore more productive) employees.

At the BVA Nudge Unit, all our projects creating interventions to change behaviour start with an ethnographic study, to objectively understand the barriers and drivers of the desired behaviour. We will often supplement this with other research techniques and data analysis, but recognise that anything that involves speaking to consumers will largely only give us a read on their rational, system-2 motivations (and post-rationalisations).

For example, in a recent project for a train company where we wanted to influence passenger behaviour, our research used three sources: objective aggregated passenger data; observation via ethnography; and interviews with railway employees (drivers, conductors and station staff). Speaking to passengers gave us very little information of use – commuting is a quintessentially system-1, habit-driven behaviour, so passengers could not give any accurate insight into their actions. But some railway employees had over 30 years of seeing first-hand the irrationalities of passenger behaviour, and their insights were invaluable to designing our solutions.

In the anti-tobacco example, it is impossible to know whether we would have achieved the PSA targets by continuing to simply ask smokers about why they smoked. We certainly would never have got to the insights about why they found it so hard to quit, nor the impact on their families – because smokers weren't consciously aware of these factors, and could not accurately tell us about them.

As a result, I strongly doubt we would have saved so many lives. Post-rationalisation truly is dangerous.

CHAPTER 20
Behavioural Science and Your Customers
WHAT TO DO NOW

I N THIS PART, we have seen how behavioural science helps businesses better understand (and therefore better influence) customers because:

- when speaking to customers, much of what they tell you will be system-2-based post-rationalisations, and this is largely what traditional market research uncovers;

- the system-1 biases and heuristics that influence a decision to purchase will often be unconscious, and not revealed by simply asking people to account for, or predict, behaviour;

- in the business-to-business (B2B) world, emotional and irrational drivers of decision-making are as important as elsewhere, and in all contexts most purchase decisions are based on minimising risk, rather than maximising gain;

- in most categories, there will be many more of these purchase satisficers than maximisers – who are also more loyal – and so efforts to understand customers should be focused on helping them make easy, good enough, purchase decisions.

Consequently, there are a number of more effective ways to use behavioural science to better understand your customers, and grow your business:

- do not rely on traditional market research methods alone – where possible, embed test-tube behaviours to generate hypotheses for testing via a mixed approach;

- the best way to reveal external influences on purchase decision-making (including marketing) is to recreate the context of the decision as closely as possible, and run experiments using representative samples (focusing on representativeness rather than sample size);

- use tools that better reveal the subconscious associations that drive purchase, such as implicit research and sentiment analysis – especially for businesses that are not able to experiment in real-world or digital environments;

- many insights can be gained from simply observing your customers behaviour objectively, e.g. through ethnographic approaches, or gathering data from your frontline customer-facing staff.

PART
SIX

Behavioural Science for
Better Marketing

CHAPTER 21

The Myth of the Rational Consumer – How Behavioural Science Explains How Marketing Works

Homer ignores most marketing

I N O N E O F my favourite episodes of *The Simpsons*,[207] Homer is driving along a highway.

"It's the first of the month!" says Homer, excitedly. "New billboard day!"

Homer screeches to a halt next to every billboard on the highway, causing multiple accidents, and carefully reads each advertising message.

"Yes, sir, Mr Billboard Man!" he says, saluting them in turn. When he arrives at work in the nuclear power plant, we see Homer has bought every one of the products he saw on the roadside ads – including unusual items like a box of English muffins and a bag of monosodium glutamate.

It is funny because we know that this is not how people normally respond to advertising, but Homer is so easily influenced he couldn't resist. There simply isn't sufficient time or interest for most consumers to absorb and process the information on first viewing, the way Homer does.

Think about your own behaviour as a consumer for a second. When was the last time you saw an ad for something and immediately went into the

---

207 *Homie the Clown*, from the sixth season.

store, or online, to buy it as a *direct* result? It may have reminded you to buy something ("damn it, I nearly forgot the milk!"), but I would wager that a tiny proportion of the items you buy immediately follows seeing an ad.

In fact, the majority of ads get totally ignored by most consumers. We saw in the last chapter how Mike Follett, from Lumen Research, and colleagues are using world-leading eye tracking research to see whether people are looking at ads, and to build predictive attention models.

Their data shows that, on average, only 75% of people exposed to a print ad look at it once, for an average of two seconds. In digital, only 20% of online viewable ads are looked at by each user, for an average of 1.3 seconds.

Saliency is therefore incredibly important.[208] One of the greatest ever copywriters and original 'Mad Men', Bob Levenson, once said: "Most people ignore advertising because advertising ignores most people."

This is why you frequently hear people claim that advertising doesn't work on them, and is the genesis of famous quotes like: "Half the money I spend on advertising is wasted; the trouble is I don't know which half."[209]

And yet the UK advertising industry was worth over £21bn in 2016,[210] despite business decision-makers often having little evidence of effectiveness. Only recently has behavioural science given us the framework to understand exactly how most advertising and marketing works.[211]

Direct (behavioural) marketing

Direct marketing is perhaps an exception, as it has an evidence-based framework for effectiveness. My first full-time job was as a graduate in the media department of a direct marketing agency, and was, in some ways, the most behavioural job I ever had.

My job was to analyse response data for our clients. I spent a lot of time in Excel spreadsheets finding out how many people called the phone numbers on ads, to assess return on investment (measured in terms of cost per response (CPR)) of the ads we bought.

---

208 Described on page 14.
209 Often attributed to American industrialist John Wanamaker, but the true origins are disputed.
210 AA/WARC Expenditure Report.
211 Amos Tversky, late research partner of Daniel Kahneman, once said that he "merely studied in a systematic way things about behaviour that were already known to advertisers and used-car salesmen."

I was directly analysing the impact our ads were having on behaviour.

Consistent with a test-tube approach, we experimented to find the impact of different variables. My analysis would look at the size of press ads, colour versus black and white, position in the paper (early pages generally tend to do better than later),[212] as well as what type of person responded to which ad. For TV, we would look at channels, time of day, programmes, position in the ad break, and length of ad. We would test all of these to find the most effective titles, channels, positions and formats to deliver the best CPR.

David Ogilvy, founder of global advertising agency Ogilvy and Mather – another of the original 'Mad Men' – also started out in direct marketing (calling it his "first love and secret weapon"), and saw it as an inherent advantage for the medium. "Testing is the name of the game," he said. "You can test every variable … and determine exactly its effect on your sales."[213]

One of my clients sold funeral plans, with ads featuring Michael Parkinson and June Whitfield. I could tell you whether June performed better than Parky in the morning, and who would fare better during a repeat of *Inspector Morse*.

Suffice to say, this kind of knowledge did not make me one of advertising's cool kids – but it did make me good at my job.

The media planners and buyers would then use this data to assess whether to continue putting ads in a paper or station, buy smaller/shorter/bigger/longer ads, and to negotiate with sales reps, depending on the target CPR for that client. This would deliver a provable business benefit, to both the agency and the client, by increasing profitability.

Referring back to the three criteria for a behavioural business from chapter 1: we were using data to build an accurate picture of what worked; we verified it through experimentation; and we had hard data on what was happening, using data based on actual behaviour (people picking up the phone).[214] There was a clear, direct link between our decisions as a business

---

212 With the exception of the back page, which is the second most read, and (for some clients) the sport section. One of our clients – the direct DIY retailer ScrewFix – only advertised in the sport pages. They had found that 'white van man' read the sport section much more intently than the rest of the paper. Data supported stereotypes in this instance.

213 *Ogilvy on Advertising,* Pan (1983). Interestingly, Ogilvy UK vice-chairman and behavioural science advocate, Rory Sutherland, also started out as a direct marketer, which suggests that it may be some kind of gateway drug for behavioural science practitioners.

214 These methodologies are not perfect of course. By only looking at responses, not actual sales, we were not analysing overall profitability (although good direct marketing businesses assess this also). TV direct response analysis often relied on time-stamped data, i.e. seeing how

and behavioural outcomes, and test-tube behaviours were engrained into day-to-day habits.

Subsequently, I worked for a number of brand marketing clients – advertisers who did not have a direct response mechanism on their ads (e.g. a phone number or website address). Looking to find scientific evidence of effectiveness, I asked colleagues how they knew these ads worked without knowing whether people responded to them. They pointed me to brand tracking studies – as we saw in part five, these have little to no relationship with actual purchasing behaviour – and everyone (clients included) seemed happy enough to go along with this in the absence of any better data.

Having come from a business where we were testing, learning and adapting based on accurate measures of behaviour, I found this baffling.

Shouldn't all marketing communications be about driving changes in behaviour – specifically, getting people to buy products and services? Shouldn't everything we say to consumers be about getting them to do something, and not just think about it?

Focus on what you should measure, not what you can measure

Based on my experience, and that of experts I interviewed for this book, this is another example of business decision-makers exhibiting confirmation bias.[215] Many marketers seemingly don't understand *how consumers buy* (because they assume they are in system-2 mode), and therefore *how they can influence them.*

In the marketing industry, the model I frequently saw used to plan brand campaigns was called AIDA: awareness, interest, desire, action. To drive sales, the model posited, people must be made aware of a product/ service, become interested, desire it, and then they will act. It is often shown as a marketing funnel, with awareness at the top, and consumers being funnelled through to the bottom.

The marketing funnel, in its simplest form, assumed that before buying a product (if that's your goal) a person needs to be aware of it, have an

---

many calls came in within a certain window (typically ten minutes) of an ad running. This ignores the fact that some people write down numbers to call later.
215 Explained on page 143.

interest, and desire it – only then will they act (purchase). This AIDA model therefore dictated that marketing had to perform these functions (or, more commonly, one of them – usually awareness), and each channel performed a corresponding role.

The trouble is, it's nonsense. People do not typically behave in this rational, linear fashion. The AIDA model suggests that we should assume consumers put the same amount of thought into buying a chocolate bar as buying a house, when one is clearly a more instinctive, system-1 decision than the other. As we saw in part five, even when making multi-million-pound business decisions people are, if anything, *more* emotional and *less* rational than deciding what to buy in the supermarket. Instinctive, nonconscious associations are hugely important in guiding our purchase decisions.

"There is a strong belief in the industry that changing attitudes leads to behaviour change," says Kate Waters. "When actually the reverse is true. Even though there is so much evidence to the contrary, the 'persuasion shift' model of advertising is deeply embedded. Behavioural science gives us both a better evidence base and sometimes leads to more creative solutions, as a source of inspiration for thinking about a brand in a different way."

This persuasion shift model persists because businesses can easily measure delivery of marketing (through TV ratings, readership figures, and the like) – the media industry wouldn't exist if it could not show value – and by simply asking people if they saw it (measuring awareness and interest). We saw in the last part that this is a deeply flawed approach due to consumers' tendency to post-rationalise and otherwise tell stories in research.

For a lot of marketers, simple correlation in the data is enough; consumers saw an ad on this date, sales went up, ergo the marketing worked. This is the same erroneous logic as Kahneman's Israeli fighter-pilot trainers from chapter 1, and there is little incentive to challenge it. If you set the bar low, then it is easier to show success to the boss.

The majority of marketing or media briefs I received in my agency career had the priority, or sole, objective to raise awareness. However, I'm aware Canada exists – that tells you nothing about whether or not I intend to visit. In most cases, the brief was addressing largely system-1, choice-satisficing purchase decisions, so only raising awareness would have little to negligible effect on behaviour. In those circumstances, the brief (and our response to it) was improved simply by asking *why*.

Why do you want to raise awareness? What do you want people to do as a result of seeing this ad? Simple questions, but surprisingly often they hadn't been considered. Asking was necessary to challenge the assumption that (largely disinterested) consumers who saw the ad would simply rush to the nearest store, like Homer buying his muffins.

It is why ads still get produced with lengthy phone numbers or URLs (calls to action in industry parlance) that are too small to read, or on roadside posters where people have two seconds to digest the information. Or, in the case of one campaign I worked on for a new telephone service which was not yet fully staffed (despite the ads already being booked), we were briefed to run TV ads in the middle of the night so as not to flood the service. We were actively trying *not* to drive behaviour!

Oliver Payne, founder of behavioural communications agency The Hunting Dynasty and author of *Inspiring Sustainable Behaviour: 19 Ways to Ask for Change,* agrees that awareness is necessary but not sufficient: "Awareness is not itself an endgame, but the form in which people become aware is important, in terms of how psychologically distant or proximal it is to the behaviour. It is a case of getting your audience to visualise the how or the why of the behaviour. You can get a positive value for awareness that doesn't result in action further down the line – and one that does."

By giving us a more accurate view of how customers buy, behavioural science provides a better framework for effective marketing, as well as how and where to focus marketing measurement. Further, there is a group of academics and marketing 'heretics' who have taken the work of behavioural scientists and sought to explain how it specifically applies to marketing. They created a new discipline in the process: marketing science.

The marketing science heretics

The south Australian city of Adelaide is surrounded by beautiful beaches and award-winning vineyards. At first glance, this might seem an unusual place for a mini-enlightenment, but this is effectively what has happened in the last ten years at the University of South Australia's Ehrenberg-Bass Institute for Marketing Science.

Professor Byron Sharp leads the institute. Working with leading global brands evaluating marketing campaigns, his team have built on ground-breaking work by Andrew Ehrenberg and colleagues from the 20th century. In his book *How Brands Grow*, and its sequel, Sharp and colleagues simply explain how marketing (and advertising in particular) works, using the robust, scientifically evaluated evidence base they have accumulated.

Sharp rejects the argument that marketing (and advertising) must be purely creative, and cannot be advanced through adopting a scientific approach. Marketing is not a purely creative endeavour (like art), he argues, because it has the specific goal of influencing behaviour – usually to buy a specific product or service.

Marketing is more like architecture, he says. An architect like Frank Lloyd Wright could create a beautiful house, which has obvious aesthetic and creative value, but if it didn't obey the laws of physics, it would fall down. Ultimately, without a scientific foundation to Wright's creativity, the house would be useless.

Similarly, a marketing campaign that doesn't obey the observable and provable laws of marketing and behavioural science will not change behaviour. Consumers will not be influenced, and nothing will be sold. As marketing, it is wasted effort.

And yet…

In the marketing and communications industry, like the rest of business, far too little work has a scientific foundation. In fact, examples like the AIDA model show that most received wisdom runs directly contrary to evidence. Like doctors who practised blood-letting for hundreds of years before it was proven to be harmful, marketers and communicators persist in using out-dated, collective beliefs. The work of Sharp and others are helping to change things, but test-tube behaviours in marketing are still far too rare.

Some examples from my own experience:

- marketers often assume their brand is unique, and so marketing activity must be planned from scratch every time (wrong);

- marketers rush to discovery, spending all their budgets in one go with little to no pre-testing (wrong);

- when they do test, they assume consumers will accurately predict how they will behave in the real world (also wrong);

- and marketers assume that people care enough about their brand to loyally purchase it over all others (almost always wrong), will excitedly tell their friends about it (almost never) and will want to engage with it on social media (very, very rarely).

So how does marketing and advertising work in reality?

Sharp puts it simply: "Neuroscience and psychology [aka behavioural science] have recently advanced our understanding of how memories and brains work. These discoveries have important implications for advertising, because advertising works by creating and refreshing memories. It is now known that much thinking and decision-making is non-conscious and emotional. Yet traditional theories of advertising are based on a dated view that we are usually rational (occasionally emotional) decision-makers, with near perfect memories."[216]

Hannah Lewis, founder of Mindmafia.com and Behave London, a behavioural consultancy specialising in the financial industry, argues that this is the true value of behavioural science in marketing: "The biggest application has been showing people that their traditional way of approaching marketing is wrong. If you make the product more interesting to people, the product sells itself. It encourages you to structure solutions as workable, or sellable."

"Behavioural science helps put advertising back in its box," says Kate Waters. "We in the industry think of brands in a certain way, but consumers do not."

From this understanding and their research on how to create and refresh memories (aka mental availability),[217] Sharp and colleagues have derived a set of provable laws that marketers can apply to ensure marketing communications work. In the next chapter, we shall see how this helps businesses create brands that help people buy, and in the subsequent chapter, how to market those brands effectively.

In the same Simpsons episode referenced at the start of this chapter, Homer experiences a more subtle, and more realistic, influence of advertising on mental availability. One of the roadside billboard posters is an ad for TV entertainer Krusty's new academic institution (and tax write-off), his branded Clown College.

"Clown College?" says Homer. "Pfft. You can't eat that."

Later, we see the slow, subconscious influence of the ad is such that Homer starts hallucinating his colleagues and family in clownface makeup. At dinner with his family, he re-shapes his mashed potato as a circus tent, in a parody of the famous scene from *Close Encounters of the Third Kind*.

---

216   *How Brands Grow*, Oxford University Press, (2010).

217   See page 14.

"That's it!" Homer says, standing up suddenly. "You people have held me back long enough! I'm going to Clown College!"[218]

Behavioural science, and the work of Professor Sharp and colleagues, shows this is probably much closer to how advertising works on our Homer-like brains than we think.

---

218 Bart's response is: "I don't think any of us expected him to say that."

CHAPTER 22

Brands as Heuristics – What Behavioural Science Tells Us About Brands

B RANDS ARE HUGELY important aids to decision-making, as we established in chapter 18.

If marketing science (derived from behavioural science) tells us that most advertising works by creating greater mental availability – creating largely subconscious associations with products and services – what does this mean for brands? Are brands simply a collection of memories? And how do these affect the decision to purchase?

If we think of the role heuristics – mental shortcuts – play in our lives (they aid us with complex decision-making), then the simplest explanation of the role of brands is this: they are heuristics that aid us in our purchasing of goods and services. And as heuristics comprised of a collection of memories and associations, the role of marketing is to build those associations in a way that makes those products and services cognitively easier to buy.

Think back to our example in part five: making a purchase in a foreign supermarket. When we are in a supermarket in our own country, the brands we see there will have a whole raft of associations, many of which will be nonconscious. When we see a brand we recognise, those associations come to mind, and if they meet our criteria for purchase, we buy. The brand has acted as a mental shortcut to aid our purchasing decision, i.e. as a heuristic, and allowed us to choice satisfice. In the rest of this chapter we'll stress test the hypothesis that brands operate as heuristics, and what behavioural science can tell us about building those associations.

At this point, you might be considering some of the best-known brands and thinking: surely they are more important than simply a collection of memories? If you are responsible for your business's brand, you might be experiencing an existential crisis, thinking that the age of the brand is over because they cease to have relevance in a meaningful way.

I put this question to Richard Shotton, who replied: "If you believe that brands are mental shortcuts, and the world is becoming more complex, then brands become more, not less, important."

This is because brands help us to choose based on our natural tendency towards loss aversion, certainty, and the avoidance of disaster – enabling us to make good enough decisions. For this, customers are often willing to pay a premium, making brand-building hugely profitable.

"In an uncertain world, when we make a decision we've got to make a trade off between the average outcome and the degree of variance," says Rory Sutherland. "In evolutionary terms to be happy we need both. It's no good going for the perfect solution if on average, one time in 100, it's fatal. My contention is this is why people pay for brands. When people buy brands, they're not being irrational. They are principally paying for low variance."

He maintains that altering perception of a product or service through branding is far cheaper than changing the reality: "You don't need to produce the thing that people claim would produce the feeling, you just have to produce something that produces the same feeling. The cheapest way of producing a desired emotion is what a business should be doing. It's not the cheapest way of producing a product, it's the cheapest way of producing the emotion which the product generates ... The advertising industry, you could say, is a way of saying, 'Don't tinker with the reality because it's expensive.' If you change the context in which the human perceives the real thing, the stimulus will be different, the emotion will be different, and the behaviour will be different ... what actually affects our behaviour isn't objective reality."

The supermarket brand Aldi knows this well. Their (much cheaper) own-label brands closely replicate the logos, colours and semiotics of better-known, established brands to make our in-store decisions as cognitively easy as possible. If it looks like a packet of Walkers crisps, it must taste like it, right?

In other words, brands help us make good enough, system-1-led purchase decisions. Which is why the foreign supermarket is such a hard problem.

Consistent brand assets

Sharp and colleagues explain the most important task for businesses trying to build the right associations with their brand: "Distinctive, consistent icons and imagery build memory associations that allow a brand to be noticed and recalled in a range of buying situations. This is a huge part of brand custodianship, yet it is often overlooked; marketers often fail to deploy a brand's distinctive assets, and in effect, they sabotage them."[219]

Duncan Smith explained to me the value of consistency: "Consistent brands allow people to use that brand or logo – any part of the brand's identity – as sort of a wonderful heuristic or shortcut to understand what you're going to get. It's because familiarity increases trust. And trust increases liking."

When thinking about the most recognisable, distinctive brands (Coca-Cola, McDonald's, Apple, the NHS), the thing they all have in common is that they are consistent. Their logos, typefaces and colour palettes have remained largely unchanged for decades.

Why is this often overlooked? Maybe marketers are humans after all, and subject to as many, if not more, behavioural biases as everyone else.

A common issue is the relentless drive for novelty in the marketing industry. According to the Institute of Practitioners in Advertising the average ad agency-client relationship has dropped from 86 months to 30 months over the last 30 years.

"A lot of the incentives are lined up in a way that rewards novelty and innovation," says Kate Waters. "When new clients go into organisations they want to make an impact, and one of the easiest ways to do that is to change something. When they do that they may forget some of the things that make brands powerful. I think it's still quite hard to win awards without something novel."

These competing incentives can be very detrimental to effectiveness. When PepsiCo brand Tropicana famously changed its distinctive branded packaging from the famous orange punctured with a straw image in 2009, its sales dropped 20% – whilst competitors all reported significant gains. It reverted back to the old packaging within six weeks.

---

219 *How Brands Grow* (2010). There is a lively debate about the difference between, and importance of, distinctiveness and differentiation principally between Sharp and Mark Ritson, adjunct professor of marketing at Melbourne Business School – but that is outside the scope of this book.

As an example of the risk of this pursuit of novelty, Waters told me a story of working as a junior ad planner on the Milky Bar chocolate account, which had for many years used the well-loved Milky Bar Kid character in its TV advertising. During a workshop the group made the collective decision to 'kill' the Milky Bar kid – those working on the account had grown bored with this powerful brand asset and wanted to create something new. Fortunately, the decision later passed the desk of a senior brand custodian, who unceremoniously rejected the idea and told them to go back to the drawing board.

To combat this novelty bias, Waters cites John Bartle's[220] mantra of the importance of "imaginative repetition": "It's about taking core assets and repeatedly embedding them and reinforcing them. Imagination is about cutting through, keeping the conversation fresh, and being creative with it. Doing the things you have to, but having the imagination to make it really great."

As with Sharp's architecture analogy – it is possible to do something creative and fresh, whilst still making a functioning building.[221]

Be distinctive

The other task Sharp and colleagues highlight for creating effective brand associations is distinctiveness – in effect, creating the saliency required to get brands "noticed and remembered", as Eaon Pritchard puts it. Pritchard defines the task of creating distinctive brand assets as making "the novel familiar, and the familiar novel", and insights from behavioural science are hugely important here also.

Oliver Payne talked to me about the extraordinary mental architecture many brands have built over time, and the importance of understanding where a brand sits in that architecture. "A zero alcohol beer has a very different mental architecture than a traditional alcoholic beer, because there is a much longer heritage of alcoholic beer," he says. "Often the architecture

---

220 Co-founder of advertising agency Bartle Bogle Hegarty (BBH).
221 Weirdly, Sharp seems very critical and sceptical of behavioural science. In the Account Planning Group book, *Eat Your Greens,* he seems to suggest that it in some way detracts (or distracts) from a focus on physical and mental availability, despite being fundamental to the approach. His conclusion is: "do tests to see if specific nudges can do what you hope they will do." Which, as advocated in this book, is all any reputable behavioural science practitioner would do anyway!

requires there to be a shared cultural understanding. We like story-telling and novelty, and a story works because it differs from the norm – but the norm has to be shared.

"Brands have to encode a mental model in the mind of consumers that is as much in their favour as possible – and ensure it is as close to the desired action as possible, and effortlessly retrievable."

As we have seen throughout this book, these associations, stories and feelings that make a brand distinctive (or not) are largely subconscious. In part five, we saw how implicit research techniques and experimentation can allow marketers to effectively understand what creates this saliency – scientifically.

Sam Tatam, consulting partner at Ogilvy Consulting, gave me an example of how Ogilvy Australia used behavioural science to arrive at the most distinctive messaging for a KFC campaign at a relatively low cost.

The KFC offer was a simple (and relatively indistinct) one: chips for $1. Building on the consistent KFC brand assets in the ad (logo, typeface etc.), they wanted to find the most effective way to articulate this offer. Using different behavioural biases, they identified a remarkable 90 different articulations of the control message ('chips for $1'). Narrowing this down to eight, they tested these via Facebook ads served to KFC fans, as well as fans of other competing fast food chains, with a limited media spend.

Based on the engagement rates of these ads, they could determine which message would work best across the entire campaign.

The winner? 'Chips for $1. Limited to four per customer.'

This was 37% more effective than the control ad and, used in a radio ad in a test market, resulted in a 56% increase in average total chip sales.

This clever evocation of scarcity bias (our desire for things we perceive in short supply) and social norms,[222] was actually in the terms and conditions, and visible in small type in all previous advertising. Making this more salient subconsciously activated the distinctive biases and heuristics associated with the brand.

By pre-testing in a contextually relevant environment, it allowed KFC to efficiently see what worked. This meant they could spend more money putting the campaign in the right places – also critical to success, as we shall now find out.

---

222 Explained on page 10.

The importance of context: costly signalling

Marketing science research has shown that consumers care less about brands than we think – even well-known, dominant brands – and, as such, they may find it hard to distinguish between them. This is why consistency and distinctiveness are important. What can also be differentiating is *how* a brand communicates, i.e. the context or channels used.

Building mental availability of being good enough might be achieved by the act of marketing itself. One side-effect of marketing a brand, for example, is that it often requires scale to reach an audience effectively – this can appear expensive (and often is).

How is that an advantage? Because scale and expense evoke a subconscious association of 'costly signalling'. This concept, derived from evolutionary psychology, explains phenomenon like the peacock's tail (for example). By demonstrating its virility and health through a totally superfluous display, the peacock signals to the peahen that it is a suitable mate. Marketing campaigns nonconsciously evoke a similar association.

The act of spending on large scale marketing implies that a brand has scale, permanence, and security – "familiarity increases trust. And trust increases liking", as Duncan Smith says.

Rory Sutherland says that "a flower is a weed with an advertising budget." It is not simply the act of marketing, but the nature of it – being highly visible and salient, especially compared to your competitors. For small businesses, and those with limited marketing budgets, it is critical to remember that it is about *perceived* expense, not how much is actually spent. As such, (creative) quality of marketing always trumps quantity.

"If supermodels were simply attracted to men with expensive vehicles," says Sutherland, "then they'd all be going out with lorry drivers."

Eaon Pritchard quotes research from Tim Ambler and E. Ann Hollier: "High perceived advertising expense enhances an advertisement's [persuasiveness] significantly, but largely indirectly, by strengthening perceptions of brand quality."[223]

It is the seemingly superfluous nature of an expensive TV advert, a large format poster, a branded industry conference, or (for oligarchs) driving

---

223 Ambler T, Hollier EA, 'The waste in advertising is the part that works'. *Journal of Advertising Research*, 44(4), 2005, quoted in the APG book *Eat Your Greens (2018)*.

an impractical Lamborghini whilst living in Mayfair, that signals sufficient resources to trust with our money. Or, if you are a supermodel – your affection.

Consistency, distinctiveness and costly signalling: ING Direct

I first became aware of the importance of these effects when working on the launch of a new financial brand, ING Direct, in 2003. As a new product, there was no residual mental availability of the brand, because ING had no consumer presence in the UK. There was also no visible, physical manifestation of the brand (no branches) – it was a savings account available online and by telephone only.

To cut through a crowded and competitive banking marketplace, the brand needed to be distinctive, salient and visible. It achieved standout versus competitors in the newspaper 'best buy' tables and online comparison sites because the launch interest rate was the best in the market. This would convert heavy buyers of savings products – expert choice maximisers, who were high-net-worth, savvy savers – rather than the (larger) savings market in general. Longer term, these were less desirable customers because when the interest rate became less competitive they would simply switch banks. Accordingly, we christened these people 'rate tarts'.[224]

The marketing strategy needed to drive account openings amongst the mass market buyers of savings products – less-interested, savings choice-satisficers – who were typically less financially savvy, lower net worth consumers. Having initially attracted them with the high rate, they would be less likely to switch because of inertia and the easy, no strings nature of the product, and were of greater long-term value because of their potential for cross-selling future products (loans, mortgages etc.). Rate tarts were there for the high interest rate, and that only.

As a new entrant to the market with no latent trust or saliency in the brand, how could ING Direct persuade people to trust them with their life savings? Costly signalling was the answer. Our media strategy used large

---

224 In the mid-noughties, it was still possible to get instant access savings accounts with interest rates in excess of 4% with few strings attached, so the market was much larger and more competitive. The financial climate is very different at time of writing – anything in excess of 2% is now extremely rare.

format outdoor posters which, by being visible, distinctive and largely unused by the savings sector, offered huge standout and share of voice. In reality, this was actually much cheaper than TV advertising, but gave the impression of market dominance (and expense), allowing a new entrant to the market to achieve much greater bang for its buck versus established high street lenders.

The brand imagery – a large, orange lifesaver ring with the interest rate inside it – emphasised the rate and had a subconscious security association, while all ads prominently displayed the phone number and website address, a clear call to action. The campaign created by creative agency VCCP used highly distinctive brand assets, that were consistently reinforced across the entire campaign (including owned channels, such as the website).

Source: VCCP

I realised how effective this strategy had been when our first status meeting after launch was cut short, because the entire marketing team needed to help man the phones in the call centre. ING Direct achieved the annual target for new customers within eight weeks, and became the fastest growing bank in UK history – gaining over 1m customers in less than three years. And the CPR rates we achieved – even from the outdoor posters – were the best I have ever seen.

Marketing science has verified Mike Follett's insight that people are "very, very good at ignoring stuff". In this case the consistency, distinctiveness and (costly) signals were impossible to ignore.

CHAPTER 23

Marketing Science –
How Behavioural Science
Delivers Better Marketing
(and Combats Marketers'
Biases)

Mental and physical availability

I N PARTS FIVE and six, we have seen that most customers are looking to make choice satisficing, largely system-1-driven purchase decisions, and consistent, distinctive and trusted brands help them do that. For a business's marketing activity to successfully change behaviour (i.e. persuade people to make a purchase), it needs to create the right associations with that brand to make it cognitively easy to buy (mental availability), and practically easy to buy (physical availability).

Most consumers have very few brands that they feel passionately about (because we predominantly choice satisfice), and many of their associations with a brand will not be conscious. Paradoxically, if you only target potential customers who do care, the opportunity to increase sales will be minimal – as those people are most likely already buying the product.

At this stage you might be thinking that if, as Eaon Pritchard so succinctly put it, the role of brands is to be "noticed, remembered and bought", is marketing simply an arms race? That the more you spend on marketing your brand versus your competitors, using consistent brand assets and making sure your brand is available to purchase in as many places (in the real and digital worlds) as possible (i.e. create mental and physical availability), you will dominate your market?

Clearly, there is also a quality question here. Spending marketing budget indiscriminately, in an untargeted fashion, will not effectively influence behaviour because not everyone has the interest, desire or ability to purchase a particular product. If I can't drive, there's no point trying to sell me your new SUV,[225] so the minimum target audience criterion for your marketing should be drivers. Likewise if I cannot afford it – so you may want to employ a minimum income criterion too. Building mental or physical availability amongst people who have no intention or ability to buy the product is wasted effort. In any case, as Lumen's research has shown, they will likely ignore the marketing.

Having identified some basic criteria, it is very easy to fall down a rabbit-hole and become overly targeted, or niche, when marketing due to the fear (and cost) of being too broad in the approach. Efficiency of targeting is often prioritised by marketers over effectiveness, and marketers have an obsessive bias towards building archetypes, targeting meaninglessly generic demographic classifications such as millennials, or creating excessively detailed audience segmentations.

Targeting is important – but marketing science has demonstrated that building mental and physical availability amongst all possible customers in the category (especially those not already buying the product) is the most effective, efficient approach.

Precision targeting means targeting no one – or only fellow marketers

Early in my media agency career, I conducted many audience analyses for use in media planning and buying (i.e. deciding where to spend marketing budget). This involved interrogating data sources such as the Target Group Index, the UK's largest consumer survey, to build pen portraits of target audiences. I would analyse demographic characteristics of our desired audience, and identify media consumption patterns based on indices –

---

225 Unless, of course, I have some influence on the purchase decision of a driver.

that is, whether they were more likely to watch certain TV shows, or read certain newspapers, than the general population.

Trawling through big cross-tabulations of data looking for outliers to bring to life in a PowerPoint presentation, I would illustrate the 'typical' customer with Google image search results alongside statements like: "Our target audience are 35–44-year-olds who mostly live in the South East, watch *Friends* and like nights out at the Yates' Wine Lodge." This would dictate media strategy, and in many cases creative and messaging strategy too.

Often this used survey data about whether people had bought the product. Aside from the flaws in analysing claimed versus actual behaviour, the data would be skewed to heavier buyers who were more likely to consciously recall buying the product.

It also meant our archetypical audience member was an average of multiple variables, which is meaningless. In a famous example, when the Australian Bureau of Statistics release their annual census data they highlight the typical or average Australian. In 2015, that person didn't exist – there was not a single person in the country who fitted the criteria.[226]

Oliver Payne also points out that reducing targeting to individuals or archetypes ignores important social influences on behaviour: "We should focus on social interactions rather than individual archetypes. Otherwise it is like studying medicine but totally ignoring viruses."

When I met Richard Shotton we discussed how, with a richer understanding of human behaviour, it becomes clear this kind of targeting approach is not only flawed, but dangerously wrong-headed. Just like the toaster buyer for a consumer electronics store is a maximiser in that category, likely so is the person who makes the toaster ads.

"Most people who work in a marketing department are probably maximisers in their category, and heavy consumers," says Shotton. "So they end up crafting ads for the outliers. There is an exaggeration in marketers' minds of the importance of brands in people's lives, because their particular brand is both in a category they are interested in and they live in a bizarre world where they spend forty hours a week thinking about Velvet toilet tissue, or whatever brand it is they work on."

---

226 According to the *Sydney Morning Herald* this was the person: "You are 37, and a woman. You have a son and a daughter, aged six and nine. You live in a three-bedroom, free-standing house. You have about $200,000 still to pay on your mortgage. You are 5' 4" (162cm) tall, in the old measure. You weigh 71.1kg. This gives you a body mass index of about 27, which is technically (sorry) overweight. Your family, at some point, came from somewhere in Britain (most likely England). However, you and both of your parents were born in Australia."

If marketers do consider themselves representative of customers, they also run the risk that they consider brand purpose (i.e. a brand communicating its stance on ethical or social issues with a view to making it more attractive) as an effective strategy for driving sales.

But this is a very conscious reason for buying and, as such, only applies to maximisers. Shotton sees this as an example of wishful seeing, or finding truths where none exist.

"Sometimes there is a kind of shame felt by marketers about selling, that it is beneath them," he says. "Which I think is silly. But because of that they look for other reasons why they have engaged in a worthwhile career, which is why we make over-use of purpose. Not that there is anything wrong with purpose – but some of the research behind it is patently flawed. There is purpose in marketing in itself, and we don't talk about that enough. My dispute with purpose is not that brands shouldn't behave in an ethical manner – it's that they shouldn't do it purely to sell a few more bottles of shampoo."

Imbuing brands with purposes beyond what they actually do demonstrates a biased view that our innate characteristics as humans have a significant bearing on what we buy. As largely disloyal, disinterested purchasers looking to make good enough purchase decisions, what is more important in that moment of purchase is often the context of that decision. By ignoring this, marketers are committing the fundamental attribution error.[227]

In business, there is a simple way to stop your marketing team falling prey to these errors. Simply put up a large visible sign in the marketing department saying: YOU ARE NOT THE TARGET AUDIENCE.

Focus on light buyers

In *How Brands Grow,* Sharp et al. illustrate the importance of not only targeting choice-maximising brand loyalists using the example of the most well-known brand in the world: Coca-Cola. Due to the general disloyalty of most consumers, marketing science shows that the differences between people who buy Coca-Cola and Pepsi (for example) are actually very slight.

---

227 Explained on page 173.

This is because the heavy buyers of one brand (loyalists) account for a tiny proportion of all purchasers.

The graph below shows the frequency of people purchasing Coca-Cola in a year.

Percentage of UK cola buyers purchasing Coke x times, 2005

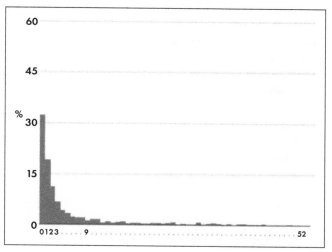

Source: TNS

The average annual consumption of Coca-Cola in the UK is 12 – once a month. But this is skewed by the few people who buy it every week, and balanced by thousands more who only buy it a few times annually. In fact, over 30% of all Coke buyers purchase it less than once a year!

"From Coca-Cola's perspective, a heavy buyer is anyone who buys herself three or more cans or bottles of Coke a year," says Sharp. "Many of us who thought we hardly ever bought Coke now turn out to be quite normal Coke buyers. Very light buyers dominate, even for Coca-Cola – which is a very large brand indeed."

In this category, even with a dominant brand like Coca-Cola, two-thirds of all Coke drinkers also drink Pepsi, Fanta, etc. This is also true of Fanta and Pepsi drinkers. Because behaviour drives attitude, perceptions of these brands are very similar for light buyers across the category (Byron Sharp describes this as "I love my Mum, and you love your Mum too"), as they are not very engaged with any brand.

Market share simply becomes a question of which brand is bought more frequently, because the vast majority of purchasers are not 100% loyal to any one brand in a category. Even a brand like Apple, which has spent millions of dollars on building a consistent and distinctive brand identity, actually has very few loyalists as a proportion of its total purchasers. But – and this is where thinking in terms of behaviour is fundamental – the high-frequency purchasers of a brand are *not* the most important target audience for marketing and growth.

It is a numbers game, and the numbers simply don't add up.

Think of it like this. The goal of marketing is to influence behaviour – in this case, ensure people are more likely to purchase Coca-Cola than competitors, and/or buy it more frequently. Marketing does this by building the right (largely subconscious) mental associations, so the brand is more likely to be noticed, remembered and bought in store. But all marketing outside of stores, that is, traditional, above-the-line marketing (including advertising), can only target *people* – not purchasing opportunities. When media buyers purchase a TV spot, they are paying to reach a certain number of people, not a certain number of visits to a store. The currencies traded by media buyers and sellers are impressions, viewers, listeners, and so on, which are all measures of people reached.

In our example, there are a very small number of people who buy Coca-Cola at high frequency. The supply and demand of media markets means these people will be very expensive to target (because of their low volume), and inefficient to do so via mass market media like TV. The light buyers of Coke are much more numerous, and therefore cheaper (and easier) to reach efficiently.

Most importantly, *the behaviour of light buyers will also be much easier to change.* If I buy a can of Coke every day, getting me to buy two a day will be very difficult; if I buy one a year, increasing that to two is a much smaller, more incremental change. Combine that with the larger numbers involved, and this is a much greater volume opportunity for a brand to grow.

Such is the importance of this work that, in early 2017, Coca-Cola abolished the position of chief marketing officer and created the new role of 'chief growth officer', following the lead of other major FMCG brands like Colgate-Palmolive, Coty and Mondelez. Speaking about this in November 2018, global vice president of creative Rodolfo Echeverria said: "Marketing in Coca-Cola is meant to drive business. The basic elements of awareness and winning awards at the Cannes Lions Festival no longer satisfies us."[228]

In short: behavioural and marketing science tells us that the cheapest, quickest and most effective way to build mental availability for a brand (and therefore grow it) via marketing is *to effectively engage as many potential purchasers of the brand as you can, and incrementally increase the chances of light buyers buying it (slightly) more frequently.*

Employing test-tube behaviours, and testing and learning what works quickly and easily, will give a business the best evidence base to successfully increase the odds of purchase.

Lots of businesses fail to do this, because those consumers who consciously care about a brand (heavy buyers) are easier to find through the (flawed) traditional research methods reliant on conscious awareness of behaviour. They are easier (but not cheaper) to target, and easier to prove that they have been reached by marketing activity. The inherent biases of marketers – specifically that they think their potential customers care about the brand as much as they do – simply compound the effect.

Ultimately marketing and advertising is a weak force, so it is important to skew the odds in your favour.

Physical availability

This chapter has primarily covered marketing to build a brand's mental availability. Physical availability is equally important, and any behavioural(ly informed) business has to make its products and services easy to buy to generate revenue.

Sharp defines physical availability as: "making a brand as easy to notice and buy as possible, for as many consumers as possible, across as wide a range of potential buying situations as possible."[229] This applies in both the digital and analogue worlds.[230]

---

228 In *Marketing Week*.
229 This includes pricing, but the behavioural science of pricing is enough to fill a book in itself, so is outside scope of this chapter. In fact there is an excellent book on it already, *The Psychology of Price*, by Leigh Caldwell.
230 As such, Sharp considers online search marketing as contributing to physical not mental availability. If you are searching for a brand, you are actively seeking it out – and so making it easy to find on Google is the same as making it easy to find on a supermarket shelf.

This may seem simple, but we saw in part two that making it easy in digital has been critical to the success of the world's largest companies, and is all too frequently taken for granted. Amazon is rapidly becoming a shop for everything and so, if a business wants to sell a physical product online, it should also be listed on Amazon to reach the widest possible market. Otherwise it is like only being for sale in a high street boutique, and not on the shelf of every Tesco, Sainsbury's and Asda in the land.

This doesn't just mean being seen in the right places, but being noticed in the right places and standing out: brand salience. In the last part, we saw technologies and tools (e.g. fake supermarkets and eye-tracking technology) for use by businesses to establish what people notice in a real-life purchasing context.

Physical availability is a necessary, but not sufficient, criteria for marketing success. If a product or service is not physically available, then no amount of mental availability in the mind of consumers will enable your brand to be bought.

I know this well from personal experience. In 2015 I was still in Australia, working for an agency buying media for the launch of a new DIY superstore called Masters. This hoped to compete with the dominant Australian DIY brand, Bunnings, which had a majority market share.

Masters had big budgets, being an offshoot of the major supermarket chain Woolworths, and we were briefed to buy high volumes of TV ads every week to advertise their latest offers ("Ladders for $10 all weekend!") in all major TV markets. Masters understood the importance of creating mental availability, and the briefs contained huge swathes copied straight out of *How Brands Grow.*

Unfortunately, our clients seemed to have ignored the chapters on physical availability. Their problem was that because of delays in planning permission and slower than expected sales, the construction schedule for new stores was sluggish. In Sydney, the largest metropolitan area, I would have to drive about 50 miles out of town from my centrally located house to get to the nearest Masters store. On that drive I would pass at least two Bunnings and numerous other smaller hardware stores.[231]

Yet we were still buying expensive, peak-time TV ads in the Sydney market, promoting deals on garden furniture and hosepipes. Those are

---

231   As it happened, I lived three doors down from an excellent local hardware store, so this was a particularly acute problem for me.

not exactly essential items, no matter how persuasive the ads, and I (like most choice-satisfying, light-buying consumers) was not going to make the (inconvenient) journey to the store. The cost savings would have been outweighed by the price of petrol for a start, and no amount of mental availability would compensate.

This was true in a number of other metropolitan markets, where store space for their massive warehouses could only be secured a long way from residential areas.

In January 2016, Woolworths announced it was selling the business, or shutting it down if no buyer could be found. It eventually accumulated losses of over A$3.2 billion over a 7-year period, and Woolworths exited the hardware market. It was regarded as one of the biggest disasters in Australian retail history.[232]

On our part, we had done nothing wrong. The media buying was exemplary, and we drove high mental availability in all markets.

Such is the price of poor physical availability – ignore it at your peril.

---

232 www.abc.net.au/news/2016-01-18/woolworths-to-exit-masters-hardware/7094858

CHAPTER 24
Behavioural Science for Better Marketing
WHAT TO DO NOW

I N THIS PART, we have seen how behavioural science helps businesses market more effectively (i.e. influence the decision to purchase) by:

- giving us a richer understanding of how to make people buy, by identifying that most customers are simply making easy, good enough purchase decisions, and that most purchase decisions are not solely rational;

- helping us understand brands better, in particular that they operate as heuristics by helping customers make these purchase decisions;

- understanding that for a brand to build the right subconscious associations to make it easier to purchase, it needs to use consistent and distinctive brand assets over time, and be seen in the right (trust-building) contexts (e.g. by costly signalling);

- concluding that for a business's marketing activity to successfully persuade people to make a purchase it needs to make the brand cognitively easy to buy (mental availability), and practically easy to buy (physical availability);

- demonstrating that it is more efficient and effective to build mental and physical availability amongst category light buyers, consistently over time;

- understanding that inherent biases amongst marketers often run contrary to scientific evidence, meaning that building consistent and distinctive brand assets is often undermined by the desire for novelty and brand purpose, and target audiences are often defined as the more rational, choice-maximising, heavy buyers.

Using this knowledge, there are a number of things you can do to make effective use of behavioural science in marketing to grow your business:

- recognise that most decisions to purchase your products and services may be driven by nonconscious processes, and so plan your marketing primarily based on insights into these using the techniques described in part five;

- employ test-tube behaviours by conducting small scale, real world tests to find out what works in a relevant context, such as via direct marketing or social media channels;

- ensure that before you start building mental availability (e.g. through advertising) you have behaviourally optimised your physical availability (i.e. made it as easy as possible for people to buy);

- consider carefully whether the definition of your target audience is influenced by your own biases, before marketing to them;

- target your category light buyers as much as possible, rather than niche audiences;

- consider the context (i.e. channels used) of your marketing activity, and whether the channels used are sufficiently trust-building;

- focus on creating distinctive brand assets (e.g. through imaginative repetition) consistently over time, rather than pursuing novelty or innovation for its own sake.

Conclusion

Beating overconfidence – accepting what we don't know

D ANIEL KAHNEMAN SAYS that if he had a magic wand, the thing he would eliminate is overconfidence.[233] In business, as elsewhere, overconfidence (and its consequence, over-optimism)[234] leads to systemic errors. Businesses – and the people making decisions for them – think they know best (or at least better than competitors) how to hire the right people, make use of technology, understand their customers, and create and sell products and services.

This flies in the face of evidence: 95% of new product launches fail,[235] and two-thirds of hires are unsuccessful. If you believe John Wanamaker, half of all marketing spend is wasted. Clearly, the majority of businesses are wildly over-optimistic in most decisions they make.

Throughout this book, I have tried to illustrate the ways in which a richer understanding of the often irrational, subconscious and intuitive drivers of human behaviour can help businesses make better decisions. But we can never eliminate our biases and heuristics – they are part of what makes us human, and critically aid our decision-making. They differentiate us both from machines and the fictional, Spock-like figure of neoclassical economic thinking.

As such, no business decision can ever be made with 100% certainty of success. Without overconfidence, no rational decision-maker would be

---

233   www.theguardian.com/books/2015/jul/18/daniel-kahneman-books-interview
234   See page 158.
235   www.inc.com/marc-emmer/95-percent-of-new-products-fail-here-are-6-steps-to-make-sure-yours-dont.html

capable of acting, as the risk in most cases would be too high. Yet it is the risks involved in business that make it worthwhile, because it is only by taking risks that a business can generate rewards – both emotional, and financial.

My intention in writing this book was to demonstrate how behavioural biases (such as overconfidence) are hugely informative and under-acknowledged in the world of business. Equally, I wanted to show that looking at the challenges businesses face with a behavioural lens can increase the chances of making a good decision – one that will benefit your business, the people who work within it, and society as a whole. To make your business a better prediction machine, and enable you, and your business, to more accurately understand and empathise with how your colleagues and customers behave, and what motivates them.

Uncertainty is a necessary corollary of all decisions. By adopting a scientific approach to employing behavioural science, businesses can become less reliant on (often groundless) confidence, and make choices based on firmer ground. Adopting test-tube behaviours – making sure that every decision you make is rooted in an evidence-based, objective understanding of human behaviour and how it applies in your specific context – removes the need to rely on bluster and gut feeling. These have their place – our gut is often right – but recognising that testing and learning, adopting a growth mindset, and learning as much from failure as success, removes the need to rely solely on (over)confidence.

When you have the evidence to back up your intuition, confidence is replaced by certainty.

Innovation is driven by learning from mistakes

At the time of writing, I have just attended the Behavioural Exchange conference, organised by the Behavioural Insights Team (BIT). Originally a small gathering of 100 or so behavioural science nerds in 2015, in 2019 over 1,200 delegates from nearly 200 countries attended. They heard from leading thinkers referenced in this book, like Professors Cass Sunstein, Dan Ariely, Katy Milkman and Sheena Iyengar; practitioners such as Kate Glazebrook and Laszlo Bock; and representatives from Facebook, Google and Uber. Issues discussed included the responsible use of data, promoting social cohesion, building better workplaces, universal basic income, artificial intelligence, fake news and disinformation, sustainability and violent crime.

There was one common theme across all topics: the importance of testing and, with it, the acknowledgement (and acceptance) that not everything tested will work. As Karl Popper said, science is a discipline where learning from failure is part of the method. In his opening address, the chief executive of the BIT, David Halpern, shared data from the Education Endowment Foundation that suggested from 185 trials, only 1 in 4 will generate scaleable solutions. However, of the government interventions the BIT have scaled, six have been estimated to have delivered value in excess of £1bn.

If by adopting test-tube behaviours we can address the most important behavioural issues facing society, then it follows that businesses can – and should – be adopting these techniques to help them solve problems. As knowledge of the real drivers of behaviour grows, so does the range of applications – and we understand just how much there is still to learn. We saw in part one that business is lagging behind government in applying solutions grounded in behavioural science, so there is much untapped potential.

When speaking with the experts I consulted in writing this book, the willingness to accept failure being as illustrative (if not more so) as success was consistent. Personally, I learnt as much from the Masters failure as from the ING Direct success described in the last part. Still, adopting a growth mindset and a culture of psychological safety that allows businesses to learn and grow from their mistakes remains the exception, rather than the norm.

The good news: businesses that do adopt this approach gain a significant competitive advantage – and are more likely to find the billion-pound solutions.

Science drives creativity – and vice versa

What was also clear from my research is that there is an inherent bias – a misconception, even – in business that using evidence from behavioural science somehow limits creativity. Whether this is simply due to associations of the word 'science',[236] or the false notion that innovative solutions derived

---

236 Which, as explained in the introduction, is a largely personal preference. I dislike the term behavioural economics as it downplays the use of rigorous evidence and experimentation.

from intuition are flawed, I can't say. But the idea that science – and the scientific method – and creativity are in opposition is a false one.

The chef Heston Blumenthal is also a fellow of the Royal Society of Chemistry. His restaurant, The Fat Duck, was voted amongst the top three in the world for seven consecutive years. All meals served there have been tested, tasted and perfected in a lab in multiple iterations before being served to customers. Despite this extremely scientific approach to cooking, no one would deny his restaurant creates innovative, memorable and creatively brilliant experiences.

As we saw in the last part, in marketing, behavioural (and marketing) science actually provides a foundational justification for creativity – that to be noticed, remembered and bought, a brand needs to leverage creative excellence. Simply providing information or making rational appeals to your customers will rarely be effective, so understanding the more emotional drivers of behaviour – and the more creative solutions needed to influence them – is essential.

The examples in this book have demonstrated that being a behavioural business necessarily generates creative, counter-intuitive solutions:

- you can decrease the length of a customer call by asking customers to slow down, rather than speed up;

- you can increase the number of packets of chips people buy by telling them they can only buy a maximum of four;

- you can increase productivity and retention by hiring people who don't think like each other, rather than people that all think the same way;

- you can increase the number of people buying through your website by offering fewer options, not more;

- you can increase the efficiency and effectiveness of advertising by buying (seemingly) more expensive media, not less.

These all generated competitive advantage, and in many cases were inexpensive, small contextual changes, verified by experimentation. The return delivered by fusing science and creativity – versus a more traditional approach – was far greater than either would achieve alone.

How to create a behavioural business

For a business to gain competitive advantage by finding these solutions, how does it generate these ideas and hypotheses for testing? We have seen multiple behavioural biases and heuristics throughout this book, and there are literally hundreds identified in research (plus many more we have not found yet). Testing all of these is inefficient, and even with machine learning tools and digital platforms, it can be expensive.

Learning from the field and drawing analogies from the work of others is a great start, and hopefully this book (and others) gives you a useful starting point. Engaging experts, tools and frameworks also helps businesses generate the best hypotheses for testing.

Hiring people with an understanding of behavioural science is also much easier than it used to be. There has been huge growth in university courses in the discipline, as well as the creation of chief behavioural officers with in-house teams in banks, healthcare companies and FMCG firms. Consultancy businesses like my own are growing in size and number, and we have seen that there are now tools like Applied (in part four) and research techniques (in part five) to enable the application of best practice.

In terms of frameworks, in 2010 the UK Cabinet Office issued guidance called 'MINDSPACE',[237] whilst the BIT employ the acronym EAST (easy, attractive, social, timely) to simplify key principles for application. At my business, the Communication Science Group (CSG), we developed a unique approach to changing behaviour through communication based on international best practice, marketing science, psychology and behavioural theory. This uses a bespoke behavioural framework (COGNITION) to link contemporary psychological research with pragmatic and effective communication planning principles. This framework was used to develop the interventions that successfully delivered improvements for the UK's largest savings bank (described in part one) worth millions of pounds.

Such is the value of becoming a behavioural business. This is where creating a culture of continuous testing and learning, psychological safety, and diversity of thought (and people) comes into its own. The experiences of Silicon Valley have shown that businesses also need robust ethical

---

237 MINDSPACE is an acronym for messenger, incentives, norms, defaults, salience, priming, affect, commitment and ego. www.instituteforgovernment.org.uk/sites/default/files/publications/MINDSPACE.pdf

frameworks and tools that ensure that experimentation stays within ethical and legal boundaries. Once these fundamentals are in place, test-tube behaviours will become habits, innovation will be baked into your business, and you will have no need to be overconfident in your guesses – because they are no longer guesses.

A business is not overconfident if it has staff that are happy and motivated, products and services that are easy to use, and brands and marketing that are driving people to purchase.

More than just being in the behaviour business – that business will be successful, profitable and market-leading.

And its confidence will be wholly justified.

Acknowledgements

I F YOU HAVE read the book, it should be abundantly clear that the content was heavily reliant on the interviews I conducted with experts in relevant fields. Thanks therefore go to Ben Williams, Chris Hallmark, David Chalmers, David Perrott, Duncan Smith, Eaon Pritchard, Hannah Lewis, Professor Ivan Robertson, James Bloodworth, Jason Smith, Julian Harris, Kate Glazebrook, Koen Smets, Leigh Caldwell, Lucy Standing, Mark Palmer, Matthew Taylor, Mike Follett, Nick Mason, Oliver Payne, Paul Armstrong, Professor Peter Saville, Sam Tatam and Steve Thompson.

Special thanks to Richard Shotton, for his contributions, the initial recommendation and advice on the writing process, and to Kate Waters, for her insights and originally sparking my interest in behavioural science some 15 years ago. And particular thanks to Rory Sutherland, not only for his foreword and endless quotability, but for continuing to inspire my own work and that of many other practitioners in the field. This book, and a large part of my career that informed it, would not have happened without these three people.

Thanks also goes to colleagues past and present for their support and enthusiasm, and particular thanks for feedback on the draft goes to Professor Philip Corr and Guy Champniss PhD.

I'm immensely grateful to all the contributors for their generosity in providing their time, insights and advice, and I hope you agree the book is much better for it. Certainly spending time with these friends and experts in various meeting rooms, cafes and restaurants made the writing process much more enjoyable. Without constraints of time and space I would have included more from each contributor, so if you have enjoyed this book I strongly encourage you to listen to the accompanying podcast to hear more from each of them, and others.

Thanks also to the team at Harriman House for helpful advice on editing, design and making it all happen, and to my colleagues at BVA Nudge Unit (especially Eric Singler, Scott Young, Ted Utoft, Gonzalo Lopez, Michelle Novellie and Chiara Gericke) for advice, support and tolerating my occasional frustrations.

I'd also like to thank all my friends and family for their understanding in putting up with my hermit-like behaviour over the 18 months I spent working on this book. I promise to be more sociable and less grumpy now it is complete (and writing this here will hopefully act as a powerful behavioural commitment device). I look forward to hopefully seeing more of all of you in the near future.

The most important thanks of all go to my wonderful wife Evie, who not only ensured I stayed both sane and alive whilst writing this and maintaining a demanding job, but also provided editorial and design input. Her perspective kept the book both practical, readable and grounded (I hope), and the improvements she suggested to the first draft really did polish the proverbial.

Index